LIFE IN CHRIST

LIFE IN CHRIST

BY

JULIUS TYCIAK

TRANSLATED BY

BASIL WRIGHTON

LONDON
SHEED & WARD
MCMXXXVII

NIHIL OBSTAT: ERNESTUS MESSENGER, PH.D.

CENSOR DEPUTATUS

IMPRIMATUR: L. CAN. EVANS

VIC. GEN.

WESTMONASTERII, DIE 20A.   MARTII 1937

A TRANSLATION OF

GOTTESGEHEIMNISSE DER GNADE

(COPYRIGHT: FRIEDRICH PUSTET)

PRINTED BY THE ALCUIN PRESS

WELWYN. HERTFORDSHIRE

FOR SHEED AND WARD

31 PATERNOSTER ROW, LONDON, E.C.4

FIRST PUBLISHED APRIL 1937

SECOND IMPRESSION, SEPTEMBER 1937

FOREWORD

THIS little book studies points of doctrine concerning God and Grace. It is an attempt to exploit the rich thoughts of a great theologian —Matthias Joseph Scheeben, of Cologne—and to apply them to the religious life.

The manner in which these thoughts are developed follows from Scheeben's conviction that the divine mysteries of our faith form a marvellous organic whole and that the several truths are complementary one to another. The line of exposition seeks in particular to indicate that all theological thought, as all Christian life, moves round two crucial points : the Blessed Trinity and the Holy Eucharist. But since the Holy Eucharist is the deepest revelation of the Trinity and lifts us into God's life, these two mysteries are in God's eyes but one single mystery, *the* great central point of all being and life.

The author hopes to make this still clearer in a series of similar volumes dealing with the other mysteries of faith, and further, perhaps, to draw out some hitherto undeveloped suggestions of Scheeben.

J. T.

Königshoven, Autumn 1935.

v

SUMMARY OF CONTENTS

I

SOURCES OF THE SUPERNATURAL
LIFE

The life of the Christian is founded on the life of
God. The Gospels show us this deiform character
of our spiritual life. The Christian soul therefore is
visible only to God. The life of grace is a life in
God, it rests on a communication of divine life. God
visits the soul, and so we undergo our mysterious
" insertion into God's life." The Eucharist is the
deepest expression of this community of life with
God. Seen from this angle the prayer of a child of
God is an abiding in the Lord.

I

"THE high supersubstantial unity of the divine nature, wherein Father and Son subsist in the fellowship of the Holy Ghost—a unity beyond the understanding and comprehension of all the powers that make up the bare nature of our mind—is a sublime stillness, where God dwells beyond all creatures in uncreated light. This august unity of the divine nature is full of life and fertility ; for unceasingly, out of this very unity, the Eternal Word is begotten of the Father. And through this begetting the Father knows the Son and all things in the Son ; and the Son knows the Father and all things in the Father, for they are of one nature. Out of this mutual contemplation of Father and Son in the eternal light of their brightness flows an incomparable stream of love—and that is God's Holy Spirit. And by means of the Holy Spirit and the Eternal Wisdom God stoops to each creature severally and inflames each one with His love."

What Ruysbroek, the Flemish mystic whose spiritual visions strike one like finely chiselled Gothic sculpture, here expresses as the essence

3

of Christian life, is the common patrimony, the glad, exultant avowal of all the Christian mystics : our life is in God, its roots are fast in the Ineffable. It is a mystery, wrapped round by the veil of eternity. In the Christian life a new reality breaks forth, which has its centre of gravity beyond the limits of all rational experience. Natural thought, even the highest aspirations and ambitions of the heart, can have no experience of what this new mode of being is. Our consciousness is too narrow, our ideas too arid, our experience too earth-burdened, to penetrate to that inmost silence, those mysterious depths, where a man is brought into contact with the Spirit of God. Only an inward, quiet, obedient acceptance, only a surrendering readiness for the revealing Word that descends from the bosom of the god-head, can enlarge our narrowness and attune the soul's chords to catch the rich resonance of encountering grace. But whenever we give ear to the hymn of grace that is borne to us through Scripture and living tradition, we must per-force acknowledge with amazement that God's love does indeed draw us into the inner circle of the threefold life of God, from the depths of which flows the fulness of all life.

In the supper-room, in His last great sacring

discourse, our Lord threw open the sources
from which the streams of trinitarian mysticism
were to flow henceforth through the genera-
tions of Christian spirituality. " If anyone love
Me, he will keep My word. And My Father
will love him : and We will come to him and
will make our abode with him . . . and I will
manifest Myself to him " (John 14 : 23, 21).
Even the plain and simple rhythms of the first
three Evangelists can only be understood by us
from the higher viewpoint of this great Christian reality. A secret and hidden, but on that
account all the deeper, mystic melody sounds
already through the Sermon on the Mount.
The Father in heaven is the great light, from
out of which the new life is viewed. The child
of God must be in the Father, in order to
become perfect like the Father Himself. The
words, " Be you perfect, as also your heavenly
Father is perfect" (Matt. 5 : 48), prove by themselves that the Sermon on the Mount is to be
understood not only ethically but mystically.
The following of Christ too, in the spirit of the
gospel, is no mere following, but an organic
union with Christ. It is a being born into
Christ, a growing in Him. How often our
Lord emphasized this wonderful communion
which unites Him and His—a communion

by which He actually lives in us. Jesus sees Himself and the disciples in one glance as it were : " He that heareth you heareth Me : and he that despiseth you despiseth Me " (Luke 10 : 16). But not only the apostles and disciples of the Lord are drawn into this union : even the smallest and most insignificant in the kingdom of God have their part in it. This apparently is the meaning of Christ's words : " As long as you did it to one of these My least brethren, you did it to Me " (Matt. 25 : 40). Only through Christ do we attain to the first principle of all life, which is in the Father. How the glad consciousness of this thrills through Jesus's words in His solemn prayer of thanksgiving :

" I confess to Thee, O Father,
    Lord of heaven and earth,
    because Thou hast hid these things from
      the wise and prudent,
    and hast revealed them to little ones.
    Yea, Father : for so hath it seemed good in
      Thy sight.
    All things are delivered to Me by My
      Father ;
    and no one knoweth the Son but the Father:
    neither doth any one know the Father, but
      the Son.

and he to whom it shall please the Son to reveal Him."

(Matt. 11 : 25–27).

The little ones, the children, are through the Son in the Father, they are caught up by the great revelation which embraces the depths of all life as its origin. Christian life is a very great mystery. The secrets of the supernaturalized, God-illumined soul reach down into the abyss of all life, into the silent wonders of the Thrice Holy.

But just as the triune God is beheld by none, so the man who is in God is comprehended by none. The ineffableness of the Uncreated is spread over the man who is sanctified in God. The child of God is comprehended not by the earthly spirit, but by the Holy Spirit alone : " That which is born of the Spirit is spirit. . . . The wind bloweth where it listeth, and thou hearest the sound thereof, but canst not tell whence it cometh, and whither it goeth. So is every one that is born of the Spirit " (John 3 : 6–8).

Mysterious as the wind, more deeply secret than the wonders and hidden things of the spirit, the Christian soul rests in the Spirit of God, by Him enfolded, known to Him alone. " Born of the Spirit," nurtured into flower in

7

the bosom whence all life sprang, the soul receives the infinite life-breath of God. St. Paul is the typical herald of the " spiritual man." No one has understood more deeply and ardently than he the unutterable reality—only to be realized in God—of what a Christian is spiritually. For him the Christian is the spiritual man simply. The words he finds to express this are hymnal :

" Eye hath not seen, nor ear heard,
    neither hath it entered into the heart of man,
    what things God hath prepared for them that love Him.
    But to us God hath revealed them, by His Spirit.
    For the Spirit searcheth all things, yea, the deep things of God.
    For what man knoweth the things of a man, but the spirit of a man that is in him ?
    So the things also that are of God, no man knoweth, but the Spirit of God.
    Now we have received not the spirit of this world,
    but the Spirit that is of God :
    that we may know the things that are given us from God."

(1 Cor. 2 : 9–12).

We know ! Christian life is not mere friendship
with God, not mere favour or acceptance. No,
there are mysteries aglow here ! Theology
speaks with shy reverence and reserve of a
" partaking in the divine nature." She sees in
the life of grace an assimilation, a real,
supernatural communion with God, which she
calls physico-mystical.

From the days of paradise, in the dawn of
human history, it has been man's yearning to
be like God. God wished to make man like
Himself ; with the breath of life He breathed
into man His Spirit, His divine grace. In grace
man is created to the very image of God ; and
if Adam had responded to the mystic wooing of
grace, the way of mankind would have been
a pilgrimage over heights lit bright by God's
presence. " Likeness to God " would have been
his portion ; for in that primitive grace which
was entrusted to mankind lay endless potenti-
alities of higher development. Since man however wished to be like God of his own power,
since he sought the germs of self-development
in his own ego, the divine masterwork that is
man was cast forth into the dark interregnum
of sin and pity. Yet not for ever ! The un-
imaginable, the (so to speak) impossible was
accomplished—out of sheerest, purest kindness

of God. In Christ, the new Man, the fountain that flows from God is reopened ; because of Christ, the redeemed bear again the lineaments of grace. They have in truth become " like God."

Grace, then, is a newness of the spirit, a mysterious *assimilation* to the light of eternal brightness and to the spiritual beauty of eternal love. But the wonder-world that breaks forth in grace rests on a deeply founded life of the soul in the interior of God.

Grace is the appearing of God's life in us. Created grace is the reflection of the uncreated grace which is God Himself. It is more than an elevation of being : since God gives Himself to the soul for its own, the soul is gripped by the heavenly notes that peal forth the canticle of grace within it. Grace is a vibrating in unison, a trembling and smouldering of the creature together with the divine music, holy and eternal, which rises in the august silence, the bright-darkness of the godhead ; it rests truly therefore on a mysterious *presence of God* in us.

St. Cyril of Alexandria, whose religious thought is one hymn to grace, declares that we are partakers of no cold and empty grace, but of " the very God who truly is and subsists."

With Cyril the Greek Fathers evolve a profound doctrine : that the sharing in God's nature, the supernatural assimilation with God, grows as it were out of the insertion of our being in the life, the bosom of God. The Fathers recognize the full splendour of grace as a mysterious life-giving union of our being with the infinitely glorious life of God.

So grace is not merely assimilation, not merely the presence of God in us : grace is also the being " full of God," it is a process of growth and formation out of God's depths, it is *life from God*. Yes, such full life from God that the soul is lifted into community with God's everlasting life. Thus we drink God's life from the source, receive the grace of assimilation with God not from outside, but from within. Remaining fully itself, our whole being is yet interwoven with God to its deepest roots and its furthest ramifications. Now only do we understand what is meant when Holy Scripture speaks of the divine seed that is sown in us, when we are called heirs of God and joint-heirs with Christ, and when our Lord says that we live by Him as He lives by the Father.

The Fathers of the Church see God's life as overflowing in the Holy Ghost. The Holy

Ghost is for them the infinite Breath of God, the mighty, all-enkindling flame of life. He is for them the apex, the resplendence, the ocean of the godhead, the *vita æterna*, life everlasting. To be conformed to this *vita æterna* is to be merged in the Spirit of God. But in the Spirit of God the soul partakes of all fulness of being, and the words of the prophet are verified : " Then shalt thou see and abound, and thy heart shall wonder and be enlarged : when the multitude of the sea shall be converted to thee, the strength of the gentiles shall come to thee " (Isa. 60 : 5). We become at one with God's life. All that is God's lives in the Spirit of God ; all that is God's is ours. And all that is ours is God's. For we have received the Spirit of God ; we are, as St. Paul says, " one spirit " with Him (1 Cor. 6 : 17).

Here what we have already surmised becomes clearer to us : the life of the soul can only be understood from the standpoint of God's life. For God's life is in us. Here begin depths of supernatural biology which theology herself respects as limits of her prayerful science. To be born of the Spirit is to plunge into the ineffable, into the primordial abyss of life ; and that means to put off one's mortality. In Paul's phrase, we are indeed clothed with immortality. Even though we remain wholly creatures and God the Creator, even though God's unique majesty as Creator is kept intact, still we are no longer *mere* creatures ; rather we are, as the Fathers put it, raised to a " super-creature-ly dignity and beauty."

The Fathers, and again St. Cyril of Alexandria in particular, refer us to the Holy Eucharist. Here we come in contact with the entire spiritualized Body of the Lord, which bears in Itself the source of all life. Here we eat the Bread of eternal life, which makes us one body and blood with Christ ; here we are verily lifted to the fountain of life, one body with the Body of the God-Man. " He that eateth My flesh and drinketh My blood hath everlasting life " (John 6 : 55). In virtue of the fact that the Body of the Lord, animated by the life-spirit of God, saturates our body and soul with the fulness of the divine life and Spirit, we are placed within the wondrous orbit of the inner life of the Trinity. As St. Thomas says, in the Eucharist we drink God's life as it were from the very source. We are now no longer far from God. We have come quite close to Him ; God in His very substance is nearer to us than we are to ourselves. The quickening Spirit of God takes hold of us and draws us into that

abyss of all life, of which the Psalmist sings :
" Deep calleth on deep, at the noise of Thy
flood-gates " (Ps. 41 : 8).

We rest in God, surrounded by the mysteries
of His life. We can do nothing now but throw
open our soul, in prayer and thanksgiving, that,
having drunk its fill of the divine life, it may
grow ripe to be a vessel of that life. When the
soul is overtaken by the sublime sense of this
reality, it would fain sink back wondering into
its own nothingness, it could almost shudder at
the height on which God sets it, at the glory
with which He clothes it.

Prayer is then the awakening of our consciousness of God. Therefore all true prayer is
pervaded by a deep and holy reverence for the
wonders of God in us. Prayer is at its highest an
evanescence before God the all-holy, an encom-
passing of the soul by the light of eternity. In
prayer the soul stands exposed before God's
deep-lucent eye. Then God's glance pierces
into us, that glance under which the soul is
matured towards God. But in prayer too man
experiences the warmth and tenderness of
divine love. All shuddering of the soul is after
all but the thrill that seizes us at the wonders of
God's love. Its evanescence is but a plunge into
God. Even though the soul's wings will no

longer support it, God gives it the " wings of a dove," that bear it aloft towards the light. God Himself must lay hold of us, His melodies must be allowed to ring through the inmost heart ; and man must then be silent before God. Praying, man grows dumb before the Lord. But when a man has learnt this sublime silence, when he has sunk before God's gaze into pure, still adoration : then his quiescence becomes a mute exultation, he holds his peace before the God of love, falls on his knees before love's hidden wonders, is amazed and speechless in the sight of grace. Ever then the soul is caught up in a rhythm of reverence and love, of expectation and fulfilment. Happy the man who waits : to him comes fulfilment, holy acceptance. It is as in spring—a gentle interplay of expectation and hallowed blossoming.

II

LIFE IN THE TRIUNE GOD

From all eternity the Son proceeds from the Father, through His knowledge, as " Light of Light," as the Word of His truth, the image of His substance. In grace the eternal Father utters the divine Word in our souls. He sends the Word into our hearts, that we may become children of God. Father and Son are united from all eternity in the bond of their love ; they commingle their life-streams mutually in the Holy Ghost, who is the seal and outpouring of God's love. This love fills the children of God also and takes them up into the inmost life-mystery of the godhead.

II

GOD is the God of life ! God's life, in which our new life is rooted, is the outpouring of His triune majesty, which surges up divine and omnipotent in Father, Son and Holy Ghost. God is spirit. Spirit and life are one in God. It is only with fear and trembling that we dare draw near to this mystery of abounding life, divine and spiritual. Again and again the Fathers insist that only an enlightened mind and a prayerful reverence, only a deep, adoring silence can truly know God. And yet we may speak, if only in stammering accents, of this life of the Blessed Trinity. We may speak of it because God has revealed Himself to us, because He Himself has broken the eternal silence. " His majesty would not go unwitnessed, His goodness would not go unenjoyed," says the tranquil and refined Gregory of Nyssa, the saint who sought God in the silence and obscurity of worshipping prayer.

God's life is a spirit-life : knowledge and love. God's being is so redundant with life that it subsists not in one Person alone, but in three coequal Persons. From all eternity the First

Divine Person, the Father, the Unoriginated, the fontal principle of all life, knows Himself, knows all the glory of divine being and life. And this primal Knowledge is life so pure and luminous, it is so replete with God's holy being, it is such entire reality, such sheerest actuality, that it posits a Second Divine Person—" to have life in Himself."

A symbol there is—but how weak and shadowy a symbol !—in man's knowledge. As man's knowledge expresses itself in words, so the Divine Word comes forth from the deeps of the Father's self-knowledge. " Logos " (Word) is the name that the seer St. John gave to the Only-begotten Son of the Father. He is " the brightness of His glory and the figure of His substance " (Heb. 1 : 3). In Him the Father knows Himself. In beatific rapture, the Son is the eternal countenance of the Father, truly begotten from the bosom of God. It is a wonderful issue from God, love-inflamed, this knowledge of God from which the Word, as " well-beloved Son," proceeds radiant with light. In the Son the Father possesses Himself wholly, and in the Father the Son knows Himself in all His glory. Proceeding from the Father, He is yet ever immanent in His origin.

He is very Child, since He rests in the Father,

enfolded by the cherishing mystery of God's
embrace. He is very Son, since He proceeds
from the Father as the replica of His divine
essence. " He is the rising that is ever at midday " (Bérulle). Ever blossoming forth, He is
ever at the full radiance of divine power. Holy
Scripture calls the Eternal Word " blossom "
and also " fruit." The blossom guards the
tender secrets of the flower's life, while the fruit
is symbolic of strength in repose and fulfilled
being. So, the Son is the endless flowering in
the Father's bosom, He is the dayspring from on
high, the dawn of God's youthful day. But in
Him too dwells the radiant majesty of God's
might. He is the meridian of God's life ; begotten before the daystar He walks in the
splendour of His holy place (Ps. 109 : 3). This
life which the Father is forever communicating
to His Son, all this holy plenitude which
belongs to the Son by nature, is by God's free
bounty to overflow in grace into our souls.
Theology speaks of invisible " missions," and
sees in them extensions, so to speak, of the
trinitarian life-processes, prolongations of their
pulsating rhythms into the creature, which at
God's touch will now pulsate in harmony with
Him in the wondrous orbits of the divine Processions. Then, as in a hushed sanctuary, in the

interior of the grace-endowed man are enacted the eternal Processions of the Son from the Father and of the Holy Ghost from Father and Son. Full of grace rises the morning star in our souls. The man, absorbed in Christ, living in the eternal Word, partakes of His eternal generation from the Father. Our sonship of God rests secure on the foundations of the eternal sonship of the Word. " What the Word possesses by nature, we are to possess by grace," say the Fathers.

" For of His own will hath He begotten us by the word of truth, that we might be some beginning of His creature " (Jas. 1 : 18). Thus the Christian soul proceeds with the eternal Word, gloriously, from the depths of the godhead. A true, supernatural generation is enacted here. The seed of God is planted in the soul, to mature towards God. The difference between the generation of God the Son and our generation from the Father lies in this, that the Son radiates from the Father from all eternity by necessity of His nature, while we are lifted into the mysteries of this endless life-stream only by a free act of God's overpowering love. We stand in amazement before the miracle of super-nature. We must learn again that holy amazement which seized on the first Christians whenever they heard tell of the " life " that has become ours in Christ. Although our generation is accomplished in loving freedom, it is yet so deep, so glorious, that according to the unanimous teaching of the Fathers it derives its principle, its ideal and its inward power from the eternal generation of God alone.

We are children of God by adoption, but this means far more than "adoption" among men. For human adoption is only a fiction, one man being treated as another's son. But here a life grows up in us. Yes, deeper, more vital than any earthly generation, truer and more actual is our birth from God ; for generation from God is union with the Father through Christ. The soul that is born of God rests with the Only-begotten in the bosom of the Father.

To be a child is to be little before God and to become big, to grow in Him. To be God's child, then, is to rest in His arms, to bloom with the Word of God in the Father ; it is a life within God's bright, everlasting youth. " The name of child means a springtime of life, because the truth in us does not alter and our ways are permeated with the Word. Truth is the eternal fresh flower, always the same, never varying " (Clement of Alexandria).

And as the man who is made new in the

Word comes into bloom as it were in the dawn of God's eternal day, so also he is seen in the midday brilliance of divine sunlight in the full age of Christ. " In the Word we enjoy maturity, grace unaltering. Always we are ripe in knowledge, ever young and ever tender and ever new. They must be new men, who have part with the Word. But that which has part with the Eternal, is one with Him " (Clement of Alexandria).

The enlightened soul stands ever in the inmost precincts of God, in the tabernacle of His glory. There, in the Father's holy of holies, whither no sound nor speech can penetrate, where all is " bathed in vigilant, unsleeping light " (Clement of Alexandria), the soul in common with the High Priest and Word of God acts the eternal liturgy of love. There the Father makes the countenance of His Son, bright with the rays of divine splendour, flame up in our souls, that we may be one light with Christ. There we are steeped in God's gaze. Issuing in one Word with Christ, we are embraced in the one loving gaze of the Father. The Father looks on us ! He sees us in one glance with His divine Son. It is the same holy glance of God, resting on us, that makes us live anew in the light. And this glance is entire love.

24

The Father sees us living with Christ's life. He sees in us the eternal, radiant features of His Only-begotten. To us also He says : " Thou art My beloved son ; in thee I am well pleased " (Luke 3 : 22). And we may say with Christ : " I and the Father are one " (John 10 : 30).

It is in prayer however that this intimacy with Christ becomes completely conscious. Catholic prayer is therefore a *tutoiement* to the Father in Christ. Our prayer is the prayer of the first-born : for in Christ we have the right of the first-born. As the community of Christ we stand before our Father more especially in the liturgical solemnities. Without this childlike frankness that dares to say " our Father," we cannot understand the Church's prayers. The *per Christum* of the liturgical prayers shows us the depth of our community with Christ as *ecclesia orans*.

Since we are His children, the Father loves us in one and the same love with His Son. But this love is God's essence—" God is love " (1 John 4 : 16). This purest, most glorious and beautiful of all things that are in heaven and on earth seeks to inflame us through and through, to become our most precious possession. The Father draws us deep into the Son, and the Son

c 25

draws us deep into the Father. In that moment we would fain pray with the holy visionary of Bingen : " O Eternal Father, it has pleased Thee to be inflamed with that love for us, that we might be members of Christ, created in that same love with which Thou didst beget Thine own Son before all creation in the light of Thy morning."

Immersed in this love, we become in mysterious fashion partakers of the second eternal emanation of divine life in the Holy Ghost. Between Father and Son there is a wonderful mutual relation of self-giving. The Father gives Himself wholly to the Son, the Son gives Himself wholly to the Father. This reciprocal giving, this exchange of love, is so full of divine vitality that it calls into being a second Procession in God.[1]

The love of God, which issues as from one heart of Father and Son, is of such supreme force, such transcendent reality, that it can find its resting-point only in a third divine Person, who gathers up in Himself all the vibrant rhythms of divine love. The Spirit of God is the infinite life-breath of God, the storm-wind of love, the everlasting fire on God's

[1] We regard the essence of the Holy Ghost here chiefly from the point of view of the Western Fathers. An attempt is made to utilize the ideas of the Oriental Fathers in Ch. V : " Life in the Spirit."

26

altar. " Fire " and " Love " the Church calls
Him. The Holy Ghost is the blood and the
wine of the godhead. Of His love St. Hildegard
sings :

> "Streaming river of blood! On high thou
> burstest forth ; love of God, thou over-
> flowest all things! Of all precious things the
> most precious, excelling the stars themselves,
> this is the All-loving, since it has given the kiss
> of peace to the supreme King."

The Spirit of God is the " kiss " of the Father
and the Son, the luminous bond of their union.
As the Son proceeds from the Father as Word
of knowledge, so in the Holy Spirit of love He
re-enters the Father. Here the orbit of the
divine Processions is completed in the " flaming
ardour of the Holy Ghost " (St. Hildegard of
Bingen), in the wondrous fellowship of the Holy
Spirit.

The Spirit of God is the pledge of the fellowship of Father and Son ; He is the interflow of
the streams of light, He is the sea and ocean of
love. In this unity lies all the bliss of the trinitarian life, in the Holy Ghost all the rapture of
God's being bursts forth. As the reciprocal
giving of Father and Son He is also the ultimate principle of all communicability of God to
us—the great Gift, the great Bounty.

We have seen already how the children of
God are rooted deep in the mystic fertility of
the divine life. Drawn by the Spirit into the
depths of the divine Processions, the soul must
be formed too in the Holy Spirit. Conformed
to the life of the Holy Spirit, caught in the
revolutions of divine love, the sanctified soul
becomes " a flame of love before God's throne "
(Clement of Alexandria). " The charity of God
is poured forth in our hearts, by the Holy
Ghost who is given to us " (Rom. 5 : 5).

The wonderful exchange of love between the
divine Persons, the eternal self-offering of
Father and Son, takes place now in our own
inmost souls. " Know you not that your members are the temple of the Holy Ghost, who is in
you ? " (1 Cor. 6 : 19). We are witnesses of the
profoundest, most unspeakable wonders : " for
the Spirit Himself giveth testimony to our spirit
that we are the sons of God " (Rom. 8 : 16).
That which no eye has seen and no ear has
heard, takes place in the most secret recess of
the soul. " The spark of the soul " is what the
German mystics call this tabernacle of the soul,
this hidden depth where the meeting with the
Spirit of God takes place.

The spiritual man is caught up in the whirl-
wind of God's Spirit—a divine storm sweeps

through men's souls. And this divine storm is love—love which knows no decline ! " The day of Pentecost knows no evening ; for its sun, which is love, knows no setting." (These words are inscribed over the tabernacle of a Rhineland church.) A divine fire seeks to inflame us whenever we raise our hearts to God in prayer. To burn in the Holy Spirit is our Christian life. " Extinguish not the Spirit " is the admonition, then, of the Apostle of the Gentiles (1 Thess. 5 : 19). This fire of love is the almighty Creator Spirit.

In the dawn of creation the Spirit moved over the chaos. He is the loving *fiat* of God, that breathes existence and meaning into all things. The love that subsists in the Spirit is the great architectonic law of the universe, which poised the mountain-masses, set bounds to the waters, weighed the seas in its hand and resounds in the jubilant choir of the stars. The Spirit of God comes upon an ageing world and pours forth, in the spring-like vehemence of His living force, the fullest, richest life. Who can withstand His might ?

And yet—this divine fire is so luminous, so gentle, so fine. It refines souls, as gold in the fire. The Spirit of God is not a consuming, but a transfiguring fire. He is a " quickening fire "

(Hildegard of Bingen). "Sweet Refreshment"
is what Rhabanus Maurus, the poet of the
Whitsuntide hymn, calls Him. He pours out
all God's sweetness into the souls that approach
Him. He is the "sweet Guest of the soul," who
fills our hearts with God's charm. He is the
Spirit of Consolation, whose love speaks to us so
intimately that we exult in its hidden light.

III

THE THEOLOGICAL VIRTUES

As the soul through grace rests in the life of the three divine Persons, the image of the Trinity is mysteriously impressed on it. Faith, Hope and Charity are the divine forces in us which form the soul on the pattern of the Trinity. Faith is the anticipation of the beatific vision and an assimilation to the Word. Hope is a participation in the divine consciousness of self which rests in the Father. Charity is the glow of fervent union with the Spirit of God. The Theological Virtues are therefore in general the formative influences of the Christian.

III

OUR life in God is an abiding in eternal day.
Christ is the day, the noonday of divine life.
He is the sublime " centre," the *medium Sanc-
tissimae Trinitatis.* For He is the fruit of the
Father and the bud of the Holy Ghost. In the
Word, therefore, pulsates the whole system of
the triune light. Transformed in Christ, the
soul lives in the harmony of the Blessed Trinity ;
there it becomes itself an ineffable reproduction
of the most holy Three in One. It is not only
that we are caught in the stream of the divine
Processions, not only that these work mystically
in our souls : it is given to the soul, interacting
by grace with the eternal Processions, actually
to reproduce them, to reflect them within
itself.

The three Theological Virtues—Faith, Hope
and Charity—form the soul of a child of God
Trinity-wise. In the " threefold rhythm of the
virtues " (Hildegard of Bingen) the soul becomes an image of the most holy Trinity. St.
Paul sees *faith* as a being-in-Christ. The
believing man has a new centre in Christ. He is
caught up by Christ. To live by faith means to

be dead to one's self and to be risen in Christ. Out of this immersion in Christ grows the new and radiant Christ-consciousness of redeemed man. That Christ-consciousness in which a St. Paul could say : " I live, now not I, but Christ liveth in me " (Gal. 2 : 20) shines forth in a new, godlike mode of cognition. For Christ is the image of His Father. He who is in Christ is an enlightened man, a child of light. " Rise, thou that sleepest, and arise from the dead, and Christ shall enlighten thee " (Eph. 5 : 14). Faith is the sanctified man's new organ of sight. It is by faith-knowledge that, going from glory to glory, we are transformed into the image of the Lord (2 Cor. 3 : 18). Faith therefore beginning as an assent to truth, a humble submission, grows till it is a kind of suffusion with eternal light. " Rooted in truth "—" a beholding of truth through truth " —are among patristic descriptions of divine faith. As a *virtus divina infusa* (infused divine virtue) it is a created participation in God's eternal knowledge of Himself, from which the Word proceeds—an *anticipation* of the beatific vision and, even though but in the obscurity of our pilgrim state, a beginning of eternal life. By faith the soul perceives truth in the truthfulness of God Himself. In the Light we see light. Yes ! as

children of God we are conformed to the ener-
gizing stillness of divine light, where the Word
is uttered in the music of eternal love.

We are conformed to the Son, who alone rests
in the bosom of the Father. In Him we apprehend God. Not however as strangers, but as
sons. God is our inward teacher. " It is
written in the prophets," says our Lord :
" ' And they shall all be taught of God.' Every
one that hath heard of the Father and hath
learned cometh to Me. Not that any man hath
seen the Father : but He who is of God, He
hath seen the Father. Amen, amen, I say unto
you : he that believeth in Me hath everlasting
life " (John 6 : 45–47).

We are of God. We know the Father, and the
Father knows us. " In faith the soul is known
by the Father " (St. Gregory the Great). At the
same time it perceives in sacred silence the
divine Word, who is uttered in the stillness of
all eternity. The Father speaks His Word into
the receptive soul. In every act of living faith
this holy reception of God takes place, the soul
is yet more profoundly transformed into divine
light. Faith is already a mystical act. As an
anticipation of the light of glory it is the foundation, the beginning of mystical contemplation.

Mystical knowledge is the radiation of the light of faith under the gentle love-breath of the Holy Ghost.

By faith we are aware of our sonship. But being sons, we are heirs also. All that the Father has He has given to His Only-begotten Son. Since, then, we become "joint-heirs" with Christ, the glory of the Father is our very own. "All things whatsoever I have heard of My Father, I have made known to you " (John 15 : 15). So our consciousness of sonship expands into a consciousness that we are *of God*. This sense of solidarity with God is the virtue of Christian *hope*. It is a *virtus divina* : that is, a breaking forth of divine power. In hope the soul shares the Father's infinite consciousness of Himself and of His power. Hope is a repose in God, a being clasped in God, who " takes rest in His saints " (Byzantine Liturgy).

How mighty is God's consciousness of Himself ! The Father is the source of all life, all power, all glory. How His consciousness must be penetrated with sublime light, unfathomed depth, imperturbable security ! Endless riches, radiant fulness blaze in God's self-subsistence. God possesses Himself. God is life in possession of itself. To Him nothing is given—*God has* !

God's riches are God's self. All earthly plenty, all created value, is but a shadowy, infinitely remote symbol, a timid suggestion of what God possesses. And then—God's majesty ! The Scriptures proclaim it. The psalmist never tires of singing it. Higher than the heavens it spreads its lustrous reality. Infinite is the immensity of God's majesty, like the " noise of many waters " . . . and yet so quiet and deep, so unobtrusive and true, full of pure light and calm self-possession. There comes over us then a devout presentiment of the wonder-world of divine power and wisdom.

All this, all this hidden depth of primordial life has been given to the Son by the Father. Through the Son, however, we have the life of God in its source. Our own poor, tremulous experience of ourselves is immersed in God's calm security, is enlarged in God. Our hope, although not yet fulfilled in the absoluteness of everlasting possession, but walking still in the twilight of faith, is nevertheless already an echo of that unbroken, glad, secure sense of triumph with which the Father possesses Himself in the fulness of His divine Essence—He who bears life in its very spring. That is why the New Testament speaks so often of the confidence of the children of God. In God is our holy vaunt.

" He that glorieth, let him glory in the Lord "
(2 Cor. 10 : 17). Hope is our Christian pride,
pride that we are of God. The brighter our
hope and the more radiant our trust, the deeper
we rest in God. Childlike we place everything
in the holy, gentle hands of our Father. Our
trust in Him is our freedom in God.

Now we understand why the Church's
liturgy stands with such high-spirited freedom
before God ; the Church's prayer is full of this
firma spes. The Church lives on hope. Hope is
her abiding in light. Even when the Church
cries out in supplication, she knows that God
always hears her. Her prayer looks towards the
good things to come. In hope she already
possesses the future glory in germ. Hope is her
possession beginning already. It is a remark-
able thing, this fluctuation of expectancy and
fulfilment, hope and possession, in the Church's
prayer. We have only to think of the longing
expectation of Advent, which is already irradiated by the light and joy of Christmas. The
great Light has already descended and fills
all things with heavenly glory. How moving
often are the Lenten supplications—and yet the
Church knows that she is even now in the life
of the resurrection ; and these very prayers of
Lent are often of a glorified and sublime beauty.

38

In the closing period of the Church's year she sees her longing for the *return* of Christ already appeased. But in the mystery of the Eucharist especially the gates of heaven are already opened. In hope we sing the heavenly alleluia in advance. " An alleluia here, an alleluia there ! Here a hoping one, there one fulfilled " (St. Augustine).

And the *power* of hope, this tender, childlike trust, ripens out of love. When even faith has been turned into the light of vision, and hope into everlasting possession—love remains for ever. " Charity never falleth away " (1 Cor. 13 : 8). As the sanctified soul partakes by hope in the self-knowledge of the Father, and by faith in the luminous knowledge of the Son, so by *love* it is perfected in the Spirit of God. Love is a glowing and streaming forth together with the love-procession of the Holy Ghost. As heat comes from light, and light again from heat, so faith and love interpenetrate. Faith tends to glow in love, and love makes the light of faith blaze up. The deeps of faith and of love call to one another. Who can ever understand the glory of the divine virtue of love ? Even the confessions of the saints are but a stammering. When the soul is seized by love, it is stamped with the glowing seal that unites the Father and

the Son in the Holy Ghost. And even more !
The soul may then offer, together with the
Word, the eternal hymn of love to the Father.
Yes, the love of a child of God is a breath-
ing forth of the Spirit with the Word of
God.

When a soul is in the love of God, it gives
back to the Father the pledge of the Spirit
which it has received. In love the soul breathes
not only its own spirit, but the Spirit of God.
Since we are thus indwelt by the Spirit of God,
the love of God's children is radiant with the
jewels of divine love; it is no longer a mere
movement of the soul towards the Father, but,
plunged in the primal urge of God's bounteous
life-movement, it is grafted so organically
on to the Holy Ghost that, itself growing
out of the Spirit, the Spirit of God Himself
now breathes in this love.[1] The Spirit
of God now prays in it with unspeakable groan-
ings. The life of the child of God now becomes
one unbroken prayer—an everlasting prayer !
Love prays continually, even when the lips are
silent. Whoever has love, prays unceasingly,
for in love the Spirit of God Himself prays.

We touch here the very essence of prayer.
Prayer is not only an actual elevation to God,

[1] *Cf.* Kronseder : *Im Banne der Dreieinigkeit*, Ratisbon, 1933.

not only a soaring of the soul to the Father. Prayer is also a being-in-God. The saints speak of the repose in love produced by the Spirit. When the soul is immersed in God, then the Spirit Himself will pray in it. God's Love, the Holy Ghost, is ever active. " I sleep, but my heart watcheth " (Cant. 5 : 2)—says the soul then with the bride of the Canticle. God's Spirit leads the soul ever into the quiet tabernacle of love.

Issued from God, the soul ever returns in the orbit of the divine life back into the hidden depths of the godhead. How wondrous is this divine orbit—very deep, very intimate, very quiet ! Yes, deeper and quieter than all life. The high, eternal import of all life lives here. For this life God created us. " God created the soul that it might be united with Him," says Master Eckhart.

This life from God is a radiant mystery. It cannot be won by any effort. Only a " passive receptivity " (Scheeben), only an expectant quietude, open and enlarge the soul's interior for the divine birth. " All voices must have become dumb to him who would hear God's whisper" (Eckhart). As the young seed springs up overnight, as the bud opens to the light in hidden stillness, so does the divine life germinate in a

d 41

veiled intimacy. St. Mark gives our Lord's words:

" So is the kingdom of God, as if a man should cast seed into the earth, and should sleep and rise, night and day, and the seed should spring and grow up whilst he knoweth not. For the earth of itself bringeth forth fruit, first the blade, then the ear, afterwards the full corn in the ear." (Mark 4 : 26-28).

The life of a Christian is woven about with mystic things. We must renew our acquaintance with *divine* forces. The theological virtues are the real forces that shape a Catholic. Our spiritual life of to-day is so spiritually deficient, so wanting in the glow of the Spirit, because the action of self and the will of self is always thrusting itself in. God's life in us is a tender mystery. It requires to be protected, fenced round with reverence. Even our co-operation is but a gratuitous correspondence with divine life-movements which traverse us. Our co-operation is a gift from God. " If you count your merits, what else do you count but God's graces ? " (St. Augustine). " The virtues flow from the eternal light into the hemisphere of our spirit and lead the soul back to their origin " (St. Bonaventure).

We must recover our faith in the divine being

in us that precedes all action. What *we* can do, is to let God shape us : " It is not thou that shapest God ; it is God that shapes thee. If then thou art the work of God, await the hand of thy Artificer, who does all things in due season. . . . Offer Him thy heart soft and tract-able, and keep the form in which the Artificer has fashioned thee. Let thy clay be ever moist, lest thou grow hard and lose the impression of His fingers " (St. Irenaeus, Adv. Haer. iv, 39).

IV

THE EUCHARIST AND THE TRINITY

The Trinity is the root of the eucharistic mystery, and the Eucharist is the term of the overflow of God's life beyond Himself. Through the Holy Eucharist we rise to the hidden things of the trinitarian life. The Church experiences this nexus of Eucharist and Trinity in liturgical prayer.

IV

ACCORDING to a discerning remark of the wise Clement of Alexandria, God is everything to us : father, mother, nurse, educator, food, shepherd and life, knowledge, truth, light. Where else is this more deeply true than in the Holy Eucharist, that food of immortality that makes us grow into God's life ! The Holy Eucharist is the way of the triune God down to us, and it is our way up into the inner life of the Trinity.

A mysterious life-movement takes its rise in the inmost bosom of God, and finds its resting-point only in the miracle of the Eucharist. While the Father gives life to the Son, and Father and Son breathe forth life in the Holy Spirit of Their mutual love and fellowship, there stands before the bright majesty of Their divine glance from eternity to eternity that supreme act of bounteous love which we adore and venerate as the " memorial " of God's wonderful works. There the ardour of Their divine will-to-love enfolds all those who approach God in this most holy Sacrament and become one body and blood with the Body and

Blood of the Lamb of God. In the triune depths
of the godhead springs forth the stream of that
tender, radiant emotion of God which finds its
ultimate and touching expression in the eucharistic mystery. It is the emotion of love which
aims at bringing all things home to the quiet
holy of holies where Love itself is enthroned in
the bliss of eternal perfection, where the unend-
ing hymns resound in rapturous fulness of
spiritual harmonies.

The triune God is the God of love. The divine
Processions are as it were solemn processions of
light and love, vital manifestations of the divine
ocean which overflows in shining love. And
this ocean of the godhead releases all the
streams and floods of life. In gratuitous love,
love that gives itself away absolutely freely,
God wishes to pour out His fulness, to extend it
over the realm of creation. Creation, then, is
the first gleam, tender as dawn, of the mystery
of God's love. When that which was nothing is
swept into the vortex of life, the joyous presage
of a full, eternal day shines out as if in distant
lightnings. Then in holy incarnation the divine
Light itself descends. In this mystery a sacred
humanity is saturated with the personal life of
God, becoming itself in turn the source of life.
The Incarnation of the Word, His life on earth,

His great deeds of salvation, His resurrection and ascension—all this is a manifestation of the primal relations of the divine Trinity, an emergence of the divinely Alone, the flowering in this world of all God's silent wonders. And now comes the last and most unspeakable thing ! This life-movement of God, this fulness of trinitarian light, will not only enter into this time-series, it will actually, in order to be ever present to the limitations of time and space, lavish itself to the last possible extremity. God therefore enters with all His trinitarian riches into the creature, so that by communion with the Body and Blood of the God-Man He may deify men and take them up into the secret orbit of divine love.

In the eucharistic mystery God's ways and men's meet. It was at that solemn hour in the upper room at Jerusalem that our Lord in His eucharistic prayer to His Father spoke these hallowed words :

" The glory which Thou hast given Me, I have given to them : that they may be one as we also are one. I in them, and Thou in Me : that they may be made perfect in one, and the world may know that Thou hast sent Me and hast loved them, as Thou hast also loved Me." (John 17 : 22-23).

The glory which the Father gives to the Son, this royal mantle of enveloping, fatherly love, enfolds us too. " The glory of the Son takes all the faithful into the unity of the Father's glory ; the language of man's hope may be bold here, but it is not incredulous "—says St. Hilary in a magnificent conspectus which views the mysteries of the Trinity and Eucharist in one. In the Eucharist the Holy Trinity becomes so to speak *our* life. The holy Bread and the mystic Wine unite us with the Word of God, which proceeds from the mouth of the supreme Father and pours forth the fulfilling love of the Holy Ghost. Then we ourselves are steeped in the ocean of life—" we pass over into that which we receive" (St. Leo I)—we are " changed into Him of whom we partake " (St. Augustine). Here all understanding must cease and only the bold venture of prayerful faith can guide us.

The glory of the Trinity shines bright in the prayer and sacrifice of the Church. Every morning, when the Church in the light of dawn ascends the altar steps, the august countenance of God shines about her. Again and again in the Introits of Lent and the season after Pentecost we read of God's sight and of the bright countenance of the Lord. " But as for me, I will appear before Thy sight in justice : I

shall be satisfied when Thy glory shall appear "
(Introit of Friday after Second Sunday in
Lent). Holy Mass is the revelation of the glory
of the divine Word in us. In the sight of the
Lord the soul glows in the light of the eternal
generation. " Send forth Thy light and Thy
truth : they shall conduct me, and shall bring
me unto Thy holy hill, and into Thy taber-
nacles " (*Judica*).

We have seen already that the Word, since
He proceeds from the knowledge of the Father,
is the eternal brightness of God. The sacred
Host, the Body of the Lord under the form of
bread, is therefore the food of the enlightened.
The Host is to us the eucharistic Face of God,
which hides the rays of its glory beneath feeble
and yet so mysterious forms. Although the
Lord is present under the forms of bread and
wine, the consecrated Bread is more particularly the nourishment which unites us with the
Word. The shining white Host at once hides
and reveals the radiant glory of the Son of God.
That is why the Church's prayers speak so often
of light. As children of the light we receive the
nourishment of the light. As far back as the
days of the catacombs men loved to call the
Holy Eucharist light. For it is indeed the sun-
song of the Divine Word. The light-symbol is

51

interwoven with the Church's prayers, as she advances through the sacred year towards the dawn of eternity. The season of Christmas is full of the mysticism of the idea of light. The eucharistic solemnity of the Second Mass on Christmas Day, which is celebrated in the early light of daybreak, gives it classical expression in the prayer : " Grant us, we pray, Almighty God, that, bathed in the new light of Thy Word made flesh, our works may reflect the brightness of that which by faith glows in our minds."

The light is eternally young, as the Word is life immortal. The mysteries know no ageing. In the Eucharist we apprehend the life of God the ever young. In the Postcommunion on Christmas morning the Church prays : " May we be ever renewed, O Lord, by the birthday newness of this Sacrament of Him whose peerless Nativity hath driven away the old age of mankind." The sacred Bread is therefore the food of the children who inherit the everlasting, immortal life of the Word. The Eucharist is also the service, in joy and exultation, of the children and firstborn. Especially during the holy season of Easter we experience the joy of our divine sonship. Risen with Christ, in the newness of imperishable life, we crave " as newborn babes the spiritual milk." Of all those who par-

take of the holy mysteries the Church sings :
" These are the new lambs, alleluia, newly
come in haste to the fountains, they are filled
with the brightness of light, alleluia ! "

The holy gifts of the altar moreover are
thrilled through with the fulness of the Holy
Spirit's love. The fire of the Spirit glows
through them and changes them into the holy
fruit of life, as once under the breath of the
Spirit the pure flower of God sprang up in the
Virgin's womb. The sacred Body of the Lord
is a spiritualized body. The Fathers call it the
burning coal of the godhead. Glorified by the
Spirit, the Lord's Body burns in the Spirit's
glow. The Fathers compare It also to a fragrant
lily. The most holy Body of the Lord and His
divine-human Blood are filled with the fragrance of the Holy Ghost. In particular, however, the Blood that flows in the chalice is to the
Fathers a sacramental symbol of the Holy
Ghost. If it is especially the sublime countenance of the Word that shines in the sacred Host,
it is the love of the Spirit that lives in the
eucharistic Wine, in the sacred Blood of the
Lamb. In the Church's phraseology therefore
the Word is always said to be our food and the
Holy Ghost our drink. " The form of wine, as
symbol of the blood, with its fluidity, its fiery

warmth, its scent, at once strong and sweet, its power to refresh and vivify, represent to us the Holy Ghost, whose origin is an effluence from the heart of Father and Son, whose mission is an outpouring which is in itself the stream and fragrance of divine life ; it represents Him to us as the wine that flows from the Word as from a divine grape—the wine of ardent love, of refreshment, of life, and of that ecstatic bliss which, in the sacred Blood that was pressed from the human heart of the Word by the might of His love, was poured out over the world, and is now poured into us in this same Blood " (Scheeben).

In the Holy Sacrifice therefore we consummate the " festival of fire and spirit " (Armenian Liturgy) ; we drink therein from the fiery stream of the Holy Ghost, who inflamed the apostles and saints ; we are anointed with the balm of God and filled with the sweet savour of the Spirit. The Greek Liturgy has expressed this thought in a mysterious rite that takes place at Mass : before the Communion a little hot water is poured into the chalice that contains the Precious Blood, sufficient to warm It. The priest blesses the water, saying : " Blessed be the fervour of Thy saints, now and always and for ever and ever. Amen." The water is then poured in with the words : " The fervour of faith, full of the Holy Ghost." How richly this ceremony expresses the profound and sublime truth that in the " chalice of salvation " we partake of the Spirit of God. In the sacred Blood of the Lamb, filled with the sweet odour of the Holy Ghost, the hidden splendour of love is unfolded and urges our life on towards new wonders.

V

LIFE IN THE SPIRIT

By deepening our knowledge of the Holy Ghost we apprehend the whole mystery of the spiritual life. The Eastern Fathers see the fulness of the Spirit of God shining forth as the glory, the fragrance, joy, peace, patience, benignity, the eternal canticle of the godhead. From this point of view we understand also the Spirit-life of the children of God, as unfolded to us in the parting discourses of our Lord (John 14-17), as St. Paul describes it, and as the ancient Church, especially St. Augustine, experienced it. The Spirit fills the prayer of the liturgy, which is the spiritual service of the redeemed.

e

V

LIFE IN THE SPIRIT

" COME, true Light ; come, eternal Life ; come, hidden Mystery ! Come, nameless Delight ; come, Thou Ineffable ; . . . come, everlasting Exaltation !

Come, daylight without evening ; . . . come, garland of immortality ; come, royal purple of our great God !

Come, girdle gleaming like crystal, shining with the iridescence of pearls. . . .

Come, solace of my soul ; come, joy, glory, my eternal rapture !

I thank Thee, that Thou hast become one spirit with me, without darkening, without alteration or change. . . .

Never failing, Thou sheddest Thyself over the lips of my soul, overflowing with Thy abundance the fountain of my heart.

Robe that dartest lightenings, scorching the demons . . .

I thank Thee : day without evening hast Thou been to me, a sun without setting, with Thy glory Thou fillest the universe. . . .

For Thou art goodness entire, Thou art entire beauty, entire happiness.

And to Thee praise is due—to Thee, Holy Trinity, in essence One, Thou who in the Father and the Son and the Holy Ghost are praised and acknowledged and adored and venerated by the company of all the faithful, now and always and through endless ages of eternity. Amen."

In this noble hymn Simeon, the hermit poet of St. Marina near Chrysopolis, and a member of the monastic community of Studium, sings with glowing enthusiasm of the wonders of the Holy Ghost. He belongs to that great movement of Byzantine mysticism which combines the contemplative gaze—a theology instinct with light—with rapt inspiration. The mystic inwardness and yet so lucid proportions of Byzantine architecture are echoed in his hymn. Like the cupola of Hagia Sophia, the majesty of God soars high above the singer. He has been called " the New Theologos." His theology is a song of praise, it is adoration. Hymns peal through his prayerful thinking. It is as though the noble spirit of the ancient Church had here once more become a hymn, just before the great schism of the Church. All true theology is a sacred song. It is doxology, literally Theologia. A believing theology cannot choose but to be a hymn. One can really only *sing* of the

mysteries of God. This is particularly true of
the Holy Ghost. Whoever speaks of Him
" must himself have listened to the eternal
harmonies " (Möhler). Simeon calls Him
" invisible, intangible, unattainable . . . not to
be reached for all our sighing." He is the
mystery of the Blessed Trinity simply. One
cannot speak of the Holy Ghost without
acknowledging again and again that here all
speech fails. Only prayer and love have access
to the Inaccessible.

We saw how the Fathers revere the Holy
Ghost as the Fire of divine love. Incomprehensible as love is the Spirit of God. What is
more incomprehensible than love ? Is it not
the mystery of all mysteries ?

The Spirit and love can only be experienced,
undergone. Only when the interior of a man
is touched by the Spirit, when the Spirit seizes
us and sweeps us along with Him, can we taste
in wonderment of the stream of His plenitude.
St. Augustine, that saint of spirit and love,
experienced the hiddenness of this meeting with
the Spirit. It was at Ostia on the Tiber that his
silent prayer was filled with the Spirit " in a
moment of trembling intuition " and of
supreme elevation. When all that else spoke so
eloquently had become mute, when heaven and

61

earth and sea had lost their voice as it were, when his soul touched the hidden depths in an interior silence, the Spirit came upon him. From this moment " the first fruits of his mind were fastened on to God " and the seal of God remained stamped on his soul.

Ineffable as the scent of plants, which contains as it were the soul, the delicate mystery, of the flower and exhales its secret life-breath— so ineffable is the love which is the soul's noblest wonder. Ineffably, only in trembling pulsations, may a man perceive the Spirit of God, whom the Fathers call the Aroma of the godhead. The Greek Fathers above all others have immersed themselves adoringly in this *Mysterium Trinitatis* and caught the mysterious love-rhythms of the Spirit of God. To them the Holy Ghost, as Divine Love, is the wondrous splendour of glory, the exuberance of divine riches, the top and peak of the godhead. He is for them the infinitely delicate " perfume of sweetness and holiness." Because He is love divinely beautifying, the Spirit is to them perfect joy, most delightful peace. The Greek Fathers call the procession of the Holy Ghost an " outstreaming." For they see in the Spirit the culmination of the highest life-movement. But this movement, this stream of life, is to them so pervaded with sweetness, so penetrated with spiritual fervour, that they have named the Holy Ghost the " divine balm," the " oil of gladness."

The Holy Ghost is indeed the canticle of love. He is the music of the Divine Trinity, wherein sings the radiant hymn of the Word. As light refracted in the play of delicate colours, as a word articulated in a rich melody, the divine life breaks into jubilee in the Holy Spirit. The Greek Fathers understand the intimacies of the Holy Ghost : the nuances of love are revealed to them. Love, the Holy Ghost, is to them not only the communication of Father and Son—as the Latin Fathers understand Him—they see in Him rather the revelation, the exhalation of the subtlest, brightest, finest attributes of God. They have experienced the mysterious gentleness of the Spirit. The Spirit of the Lord is to them love, joy, peace, consolation, benignity, patience, thanksgiving. And yet these are merely words that hint like a far-away melody at the tender glories of the Holy Ghost.

In the patristic conception of the Holy Ghost lingers the lofty note of our Lord's farewell discourses with their glad promise of the Spirit. The words of Jesus are steeped in the holiness of the Spirit. A new spiritual reality opens out here : our Lord Himself gives us a glimpse into the hidden essence of the Paraclete and the riches of a life according to the Spirit.

It was after the eucharistic meal, when the Lord's Blood was shed in the chalice as the out-pouring of His spiritual love. With prophetic glance Jesus looks into the future, and sees His transfigured glory. His approaching Passion is the way that leads to it. For now is the prince of this world judged. " In Me he hath not anything. But that the world may know that I love the Father : and as the Father hath given Me commandment, so do I " (John 14 : 30-31). His death is a manifestation of royal love, it is a transition to His life in the glory of the Spirit. In the Supper Room Jesus anticipated not only His sacrifice of Good Friday as High Priest, but also His consummation in the Father through the Spirit. In this sense we understand our Lord's exultant words : " Now is the Son of Man glorified, and God is glorified in Him. If God is glorified in Him, God also will glorify Him in Himself, and immediately will He glorify Him " (John 13 : 31-32).

The Spirit is transfiguration. Only as One who is transfigured in the Spirit can Christ be really near to His own. Only when physical and psychological bond have been burst by the

Spirit can He insert His disciples into Himself and fill them with the glory of the Comforter. So Jesus sees in one glance His own Pentecost and that of His apostles. He sees the hour of consummation, of Pentecost, which will begin with the first Whitsunday. In that hour He will come to them in the Spirit, that is, as One glorified, as the spiritual Vine which fills its branches with its own abundant life and makes them spiritual men : " He shall glorify Me, because He shall receive of Mine and shall show it to you " (John 16 : 14). In the Spirit a new world ripens. Pentecost is the breaking forth, the beginning of Christ's return. True, it is veiled as yet, but the children of God know it through the Holy Ghost : the world itself seen in the light of Pentecost is a transfiguration, a life in Christ glorified.

The Lord Christ, as St. Paul says, is " spirit." His glorified humanity, anointed with the Spirit from the beginning, is now irradiated by the Spirit's beauty. Now at last is that manifest which in the earthly life of Jesus was veiled. Prophetically He speaks of this glorious, divinized order of things which His disciples also are to know. It is a new kind of reality, a completely ennobled kind. Our Lord's words are as the undulations of a divine hymn. They thrill with the consciousness of a world that grows out of the love and unity, the peace and joy of the Spirit.

The Spirit appears as love. " Abide in My love," says Jesus (John 15 : 9). To abide in His love is to abide in the Spirit. As the being of the glorified Saviour is love, so must the members of Jesus be love. The faithful live by love, which is God's eternal, living Spirit. Love is the new, spiritual existence of the redeemed. It is an anticipation of the glory to come : " A new commandment I give unto you : that you love one another, as I have loved you, that you also love one another. By this shall all men know that you are My disciples, if you have love one for another" (John 13 : 34–35). "This is My commandment, that you love one another, as I have loved you. Greater love than this no man hath, that a man lay down his life for his friends. You are My friends, if you do the things that I command you. I will not now call you servants : for the servant knoweth not what his lord doth. But I have called you friends : because all things, whatsoever I have heard of My Father, I have made known to you. You have not chosen Me, but I have chosen you ; and have appointed you, that you should go and should bring forth fruit ; and your fruit should remain : that whatsoever you shall ask of the Father in My name, He may give it you. These things I command you, that you love one another " (John 15 : 12–17).

The Spirit is union—communion. From the Spirit of God alone springs true communion. How wonderfully our Lord speaks of communion in God—in imperishable, eternal words ! It is always finding new and joyous expression. Because we are one, we pray in the name of Jesus. And the Father gives us His Spirit, because He loves us as children in Christ. Christ and His members are an indissoluble unity. When one prays, all pray. To ask in the name of Christ means to ask as Christ Himself. By the power of the immortal Spirit the community of the Church no longer stands distinct and separate from Christ, but rather has become the mystical Christ, to whom the Father can refuse nothing, because He assents to Christ's promise : " Amen, amen, I say to you : if you ask the Father anything in My name, He will give it you" (John 16 : 23). " In that day you shall ask in My name : and I say not to you that I will ask the Father for you. For the Father Himself loveth you, because you have loved Me and have believed that I came out from God " (John 16 : 26–27).

The Spirit is eternal, radiant joy. In the Spirit all joy dwells. The Paraclete is the river of bliss. Joy is the expression of a strong, youthful, eternal world. In the Holy Ghost dwells the triumphant invincibility of God. Visited by the Spirit, sealed by the Spirit, all the redeemed wear an immortal crown of victory. Amid the tribulations of a world that knows not God resound those words of comfort in the hearts of the faithful : " You now indeed have sorrow : but I will see you again (as glorified members in the everlasting Pentecost), and your heart shall rejoice ; and your joy no man shall take from you. . . . Ask, and you shall receive ; that your joy may be full " (John 16 : 22, 24).

God's Spirit is eternal peace. He is the peace that the world does not understand, because the Spirit of God is not comprehended. In Him the soul rests in the *pax Christi*, the peace of Christ. Just as a melody cannot be analysed, but only perceived, so the peace of God can only be known by experience. The " world " too seeks peace. Its peace, however, is but the compensation of mutually opposed forces. It is no more than a balance between disguised selfish tendencies. Imposed by external force, the peace of this world is but a remote and obscure prognostic of God's peace. The peace of Christ

however, exulting in our hearts, is the indescribable music of souls chiming in the harmonies of the Holy Spirit.

All these great, stirring realities are mani-
fested in the name that our Lord Himself gave
to the Holy Ghost. He is the " Paraclete."
The word is really untranslatable. The Paraclete is the Comforter, the fine, tender, joyful,
uniting, exultant, splendid love of God, which
no human heart can taste to the full and whose
hidden wonders are gathered together in the
blessedness of the spiritual life.

This melody of the Holy Spirit echoes
through the writings of St. Paul. It gives them
a subtle and mysterious quality and rhythm
which fill all his epistles with spiritual fervour.
We have only to think of the great hymn to
charity in 1 Cor. 13. It is a hymn of the Spirit,
the Paraclete. The charity that the Apostle
sings is the breath of the Holy Ghost. We see
clearly here what St. Paul means by love. He
sees it not so much as the mighty, creative
force ; he divines rather its tender, hidden
mystery, its spirit-mode of being. When St.
Paul says : " Charity is patient, is kind :
charity envieth not, dealeth not perversely, is
not puffed up, is not ambitious, seeketh not her
own, is not provoked to anger . . . beareth all

69

things, believeth all things, hopeth all things, endureth all things," these words, like so many others in St. Paul, are to be understood not logically, that is as mere words, but in their melodic quality, in their indefinable tones. The music of God's love quivers over the life of the spiritual man. Paul shows us the life of a child of God as movement in the subtle, spiritual vibrations of the Holy Ghost.

Christian life, as we saw, is no mere ethic. Here we recognize our new life as the perfume of the Holy Ghost. " We are the good odour of Christ" (2 Cor. 2 : 15) in the Holy Ghost. "The faithful give forth the sweet odour of resurrection," says an ancient Christian spiritual writer. The spirit of the Paraclete is wafted to us in the Apostle's wonderful passages about Him, passages which reveal the Christian life to us. Such words cannot be translated, only felt and lived:

"In all things let us exhibit ourselves as the ministers of God, in much patience, in tribulation, in necessities, in distresses, in stripes, in prisons, in seditions, in labours, in watchings, in fastings, in chastity, in knowledge, in long-suffering, in sweetness, in the Holy Ghost, in charity unfeigned" (2 Cor. 6 : 4–6).

The patient, the enduring, the suffering, the

gentle are those who love in the Holy Spirit. They are those who bless, whose law is forgiveness. The Christian's task is to dispense the blessing of God, to be a child of blessing. All suffering, all persecution is for St. Paul a manifestation of divine forces in this world, a sanctification of the sinful earth. For this reason the Christian is unconquerable. His life thrives amid persecution—it is suffering in love. " Suffering is the ecstasy of love," says Methodius of Olympus. Suffering is the power of the Spirit ; in the victim glows the Spirit. In Him we become a sacrifice of praise, " sanctified in the Holy Ghost " (Rom. 15 : 16).

And now, shed over our life, there lies an inimitable beauty of the Spirit, like an unction —a divine harmony and loveliness. Paul celebrates it in hymn-like verses :

" Put ye on therefore, as the elect of God, holy and beloved, the bowels of mercy, benignity, humility, modesty, patience :

Bearing with one another and forgiving one another, if you have a complaint against another. Even as the Lord hath forgiven you, so do you also.

But above all these things have charity, which is the bond of perfection." (Col. 3 : 12–14).

" . . . Loving one another with the charity
of brotherhood : with honour preventing
one another :

In carefulness not slothful, in spirit fervent.
Serving the Lord :

Rejoicing in hope, patient in tribulation,
instant in prayer :

Communicating to the necessities of the
saints, pursuing hospitality.

Bless them that persecute you : bless, and
curse not.

Rejoice with them that rejoice : weep with
them that weep." (Rom. 12 : 10–15).

This is no commandment, no precept ! No,
these words are written as a charismatic song
of praise. What humble, simple union is here !
Children of God, who are on fire with the
Spirit, are one life in the Spirit. They see
Christ in one another and recognize with
spiritual reverence the divine traits in souls.
Life in the Spirit is a life in the Kingdom of
Heaven, a life beyond these limits of time and
space, an existence in the glorified Lord Christ.
" God hath made us sit together in the heavenly
places " (Eph. 2 : 6). " *Our* conversation is in
heaven " (Phil. 3 : 20).

The Christian, therefore, goes through this
world with a holy reserve. All has become to

him as nothing, because Christ *is*. Weighed
against this fact, the particular values of things
sink in the scale. The forms and modes of this
life no longer matter. The world's contours
grow dim. The Christian uses things as though
he used them not. Everything, even the highest
goods of life, have become to him questionable,
relative. He lives in this world like other men,
and yet his real life is not here on earth. He
deals with the world, but he does so as though
the world were not there. If he is married, he
lives as though he were not married ; if he
mourns, his mourning is as suppressed joy ; if
he is joyful, his joy is full of that quiet, sage
serenity of the children of God, who know that
all is but a perishable symbol and allegory,
" for the fashion of this world passeth away "
(1 Cor. 7 : 31). As one dead, and awakened in
Christ, driven by the Spirit, he goes on through
these times and tides, on towards eternity,
seeking the things that are above (Col. 3 : 1).

The everlasting day of God draws nigh. The
dawn is already aglow. The Lord cometh !
The seal of the Spirit is the beginning and
earnest of the great day. The day of the Lord,
however, is the day of adoration " in spirit and
in truth " (John 4 : 23). *A Spirit of hymnody is
the Holy Ghost !* Heaven's eternal *Gloria* ! And

f   73

in the Spirit our life too becomes a sacred song before God. "Be ye filled with the Holy Spirit, speaking to yourselves in psalms and hymns and spiritual canticles, singing and making melody in your hearts to the Lord : giving thanks always for all things, in the name of our Lord Jesus Christ, to God and the Father" (Eph. 5 : 18–20). The Spirit of God is the riches of the Word, He is the Son's great prayer of thanksgiving to His Father, the eternal panegyric. In Him our life becomes a *eucharistia* in the Holy Ghost. Because of this Christians are for ever overflowing with thankfulness. Thanksgiving is the spiritual sacrifice of the Christian, the new attitude of the children of light, who are ever thrilled with the glory of living near to God. Full of gratitude, they offer to the Lord the " sacrifice of praise," " the fruit of lips confessing to His name " (Heb. 13 : 15).

That which our Lord predicted in His words of promise as the spiritual reality of the future, St. Paul found in the new life of Christians. Now he too knows how to speak of the peace of God ! Over and over again we hear of *peace and joy in the Holy Ghost*. Living in God, in the Spirit, the Christian has already entered into this everlasting peace of God—that peace the

bliss of which surpasses all understanding.
" Let the peace of Christ rejoice in your hearts,
wherein also you are called in one body " (Col.
3 : 15). This one body, built up in the Holy
Spirit, is the goal of cosmic history. It is the
consummation, and in love, peace and communion it ripens into its eternal Pentecost :
" The God of peace and of love shall be with
you. Salute one another with a holy kiss. . . .
The grace of our Lord Jesus Christ and the
charity of God and the communication of the
Holy Ghost be with you all. Amen." (2 Cor.
13 : 11–13).

The mystery of the spiritual life takes shape
for us from the words of Scripture. It is a life
in Christ glorified, exalted by the Spirit ; a life
in all the height and depth and breadth, all
the unspeakable riches of Christ : a life of love,
of peace and of gladness ! The new world that
is to come has already its beginning here. For
the ancient Church the possession of the Spirit
was the sign of a living Christian. The
Christian is a " spiritual man." Every believer
is a *pneumatikos*. In the Holy Spirit he grasps
the pledge of Christ's transfigured glory and
feels the beginning of it. For that reason the
Church, as the community of the members of
the glorified Christ who are animated by God's

Spirit, is the emergence of the coming æon.

The Church is the realm of the Holy Ghost. The age of the Spirit begins in the Church. The first Christians were profoundly conscious of this. What captivates us again and again in the picture of the early Church, is the breath of the Spirit, transfiguring all things. Early Christian literature is full of this " odour of unction." In its remote beginnings it is actually charismatic. We need only think of the Christian sybils, those unknown poets lit up by the spirit of prophecy, and their rapt speech. With sweet psalms and hymns in the joyous, animated communion of the brethren, the All-Father was celebrated—" whose thoughts are wisdom " (Odes of Solomon). An entirely new sense of life fills these men : the knowledge of their life in the Spirit. Joy thrills through the liturgical solemnities of the first Christians. Ecstatic fervour sings hymns full of peace. All becomes liturgy ! All becomes a hymn ! Singing and rejoicing in the Spirit, the word was spread abroad. How the spirit of the first Christians—this spirit of quiet, joyful, humble love, of holy meekness and fellowship, full of the high consciousness of glory—encompasses us when we read the letters of St. Ignatius of Antioch ! They are an ode to the unity and fellowship of the faithful in one body and one spirit. Christians ought to be a canticle of Christ. They ought to form a mystic choir, making concord together and praising the Father in a divine harmony through Christ. As the strings are united with the lute, so are the faithful united together, and the song of the Lord sings unanimous love in them. The Christian's life is a life in joy. St. Ignatius's heart and spirit are ever overflowing with joy. Like another St. Paul, he too is always speaking of joy. He, the prisoner, on the way to Rome, manacled to ten soldiers, going to his martyrdom—he cannot but cry out for joy. " In perfect joy " he greets " the most happy churches " which give him consolation and encouragement on his way to the place of death. For everything, even pain, is to the spiritual man a cause for rejoicing in the Spirit. He calls the church in Philadelphia one which " rejoices without ceasing in the Passion of our Lord and which is perfected in His resurrection."

The theology of the great Alexandrians and the godly wisdom of the Syrian Fathers, those singers of the Holy Ghost, affect us like the singing of hymns. For Clement of Alexandria theology is the song of the Logos, who sends forth the seven-rayed spirit of hymnody.

Ephraem the Syrian celebrated God's wisdom
in poems and fortified the true doctrine by
choirs of singers. He overcame the spurious
inspiration of heretics by the genuine spiritual
emotion of his hymns. And what praise of
God rings through the solemn silence of the
desert in the prayer and in the life of this hermit
who has caught the hallowed vibrations of the
Spirit of God !

In the West we catch these spirit-voices
especially in St. Augustine's theology of love.
Christ is the centre of his theological thought,
and his spirit is love. Love is God in us, it
is a divine illumination of the soul, a consummation in God's light. Love is the exquisite
beauty of the soul, more precious than all the
goods of this passing world. In love we advance
daily towards eternal life, full of longing for the
imperishable light which will one day envelope
us, as the light on the eternal hills. Love is the
election of the saints, He who loves is of God's
elect ; love is holiness itself, it is the great song
that fills the saints, those who run like wheeling
stars in the train of the divine Sun, rejoicing to
run their way (Ps. 18 : 6). Love is the light of
confessors, the ardour of martyrs, the nobility
of holy virgins ; it is the great structural law of
the kingdom of God. Love is " spirit, strength

and salvation." It is the fragrance of the virtues, the melody that rises from the virtues' chorus. Spiritual love is the ordering principle of the whole inner life. It is the life-giving force of the Christian soul ; love is the canticle that fills all things with hidden glory. St. Augustine speaks of its beauty in inspired words :

" Love is strength . . . love is beauty, love is delight, love is pasture, food and drink. . . . Therefore, my brethren, pursue love, the sweet and salutary bond of souls ; for without it the rich man is poor, and with it the poor man is rich. Love is patient in misfortune, moderate in good fortune, strong in suffering, glad in toil, secure in temptation, large-hearted in hospitality ; among true brethren most happy, among false brethren most patient . . . composed in the face of insults, kindly towards hatred, calm towards anger. . . . What has strength like that of love ?—strength not to avenge, but to forget ! What has faith like love's ?—faith not in folly, but in the truth ! . . .

" O love that ever burnest, love that art never quenched, O God, my love, inflame me ! "

St. Augustine is the warm-hearted saint who has perceived the full richness of love's melody. Love is to him the common life of the members of Christ in the Holy Ghost. To love one another, to " prevent one another in honour," is to propagate the Holy Ghost Himself, who is the sacred breath of the mystical body of Christ. In love we feel the " Unutterable " ; love is an entrance into the " vastness." In love we take hold of the vast riches of God. It is the pearl of great price, the buried treasure, for which the believer sacrifices everything. It forms us to the very likeness of God, for God is indeed love. Love leads us into the boundless land of the godhead, makes us like Him who encompasses all men, who makes His sun to rise over good and bad. The more a soul grows in love, the vaster it must become. Inward vastness is the mark of a soul touched by God. All contact with God occurs in love. The fulness of wisdom is poured out over him who loves. St. Augustine asserts repeatedly and emphatically that only love knows. Love is the spiritual unction which allows us to taste of God's mysteries. Yes, in love comes the tender, silent, unspeakable unclosing of God in the soul : " Something has come to life in thee which thou canst not speak in words. Before thou hadst perceived it thus as it were visibly, thou thoughtest thyself doubtless able to speak of it : but as thou perceivest Him now, thou knowest that thou canst not describe what thou perceivest : He is the Unutterable ! " In these words St. Augustine touches on the metaphysical mystery of love. It is one thing with God, ineffable, as the Ineffable Himself. But since love is God and the Spirit of God, St. Augustine dares to use such bold language about it. Not to be measured by human standards is this saying of his :

" *Love, and then do what thou wilt !* Let the root of love be within thee ; from this root only good can come." He who has love, has all things besides. Love is the fulness of them all. That is why our spiritual life is so simple. It is just love, in God and in His Spirit ! The great doctor of Hippo stresses it again and again : " Instead of many methods, have love."

But we cannot get love by any effort of our own : for it is from God. It is a gift, simply and solely. Love can only take hold of us. But this is our consolation and our joy : God has " first loved us " (1 John 4 : 19). To love, then, means to be loved by God, to let oneself be loved by God. Therein is contained our whole way to God : to surrender oneself to love. If, however, a man think that he cannot love, the words of Master Eckhardt may be applied to him : " If thou thinkest that thou canst not

love, then desire to love ; if thou canst not
even do this, then pray for a desire to love."
He who desires God, loves already. And he
who loves, lives in peace. Love makes one rest
in God. Love sings already the alleluia here and
prepares us for the " happy alleluia there."—
" Therefore let the alleluia sound on thy lips.
Singing alleluia, let us lift up our faces to the
day without end, to the land of immortality.
Let us hasten to the everlasting house. Blessed
are they that dwell in Thy house, O Lord ! They
shall praise Thee for ever and ever " (Ps. 83 : 5)
(St. Augustine).

The Church in her liturgy sings the praises
of love. Her words and sacred actions are
hallowed by the Spirit of God. How the whole
spiritual reality rises into being in the service of
the altar ! Day by day the praise of God goes
round the whole earth on the " wings of the
dawn." The sacrifice of love encompasses the
whole world. Sacrifice is a loving procession of
the multitude to God.

Let us listen now to the sacred voices of the
Liturgy. In the Liturgy of St. John Chrysostom,
after the solemn procession of the offerings and
the offertory prayer, the priest says aloud :
" Let us love one another, that we may with one
mind confess the Father, Son and Holy Ghost,

the consubstantial and indivisible Trinity." He then bows deeply three times before the holy table, kisses the sacred offerings under their veil, and prays in a low voice : " I will love Thee, O Lord, my strength, my defence, my refuge and my salvation." The choir then sings the *Credo*, which the Greeks call the " Great Doxology " and regard as a hymn of praise. While it is sung the priest lifts the veil and fans with it over the offerings, as if to symbolize the hovering of the Holy Spirit, whose sacrificial love breathes through the sacred Gifts and through all the faithful. The Holy Sacrifice is a drama of the Spirit. Constantly the prayers and hymns of the Greek Mass speak of the Holy Ghost. It is all hymning, glorifying, exulting—and what quivering fervour, what a " tremulous resonance " of hearts fills its melodies !

The Latin Mass, at the offering of the chalice, speaks of the " odour of sweetness," with which our gifts are perfumed and in which they ascend to God. " We offer Thee, O Lord, the Chalice of Salvation, beseeching Thy mercy that, in the sight of Thy divine Majesty, it may ascend with an odour of sweetness for our salvation and that of the whole world." The " mystery of faith " is what the Church calls the

Precious Blood in the chalice at the consecration. Is she thinking perhaps of all the inexpressible, incalculable things, of the hidden fragrance of faith, which ascends from the eucharistic Blood, as its inmost mystery?

We saw that the Holy Ghost is the music, the *eucharistia*, of the divine Word. In the Church's sacrifice the Word's hymn of praise, divine and human, in the Holy Ghost, sounds forth under the sacred species. Holy Mass is called a sacrifice of praise. Again and again in her liturgical hymns the Church insists on the heavenly nature of the Holy Sacrifice. We need but recall the Introits after Epiphany or the wonderful chants after Easter. Text and melody here form a whole. The nearer we approach to Pentecost, the more spiritualized, transfigured, becomes the prayer and song. The Spirit of God exults in the Church's music. How indescribable, for example, is the jubilation of the Fifth Sunday after Easter, with its extraordinary manifestation of clear-shining fervour and joyfully excited festivity:

" Lift up the voice of joy, and let it be heard, alleluia: announce it even to the ends of the earth: the Lord hath set free His people, alleluia alleluia! Shout with joy to God, all the earth: sing ye a psalm to His name, give glory to His praise " (Ps. 65 : 1–2).

Every scale of religious emotion is to be found in the chants after Easter : joy, triumph, thanksgiving, devotion, and gentle, consuming ardour. And then comes Pentecost, the great feast-day of the Spirit ! It is as if the melody revealed the Holy Ghost Himself. What suppressed power trembles in the melody of the Introit ! An urgency and increase, a mighty agitation makes us feel the rush and impetuosity of the Holy Spirit's divine force of love. Yet Pentecost is not only the impetuous strength of God—it is stillness, too, and the spring-soft budding of the seed of divine love. Here again the plain-song is the best commentary on the feast and its sacramental transaction : when the Epistle has been sung, at the second Alleluia-verse the priest and ministers kneel while the choir sings the words : *Veni, Sancte Spiritus, reple tuorum corda fidelium et tui amoris in eis ignem accende.* (" Come, O Holy Spirit, fill the hearts of Thy faithful and kindle in them the fire of Thy love.") The love of the *Creator Spiritus* is sung here with gentle devotion. We surmise the full riches, the abundance of God's love in the chanting of the words *tui amoris.* But a veritable theology of the Holy

Ghost sings the incomparable Pentecost Sequence, with its melodious rhythms which fall as the beating of the Dove's wings :

Veni, sancte Spiritus,
et emitte caelitus
lucis tuae radium.

Come, Holy Spirit, and send forth from heaven the radiance of Thy light.

Come, Father of the poor ; come, Giver of gifts ; come, Light of hearts.

Best Consoler, sweet Guest of the soul, sweet refreshment.

In labour rest, coolness in heat, comfort in tears.

O most blessed Light, fill the inmost hearts of Thy faithful.

Without Thy divine power, nothing is in man, nothing but what is harmful.

Cleanse what is soiled ; water what is dry ; heal what is wounded.

Bend what is rigid ; chafe what is cold ; straighten what is crooked.

Grant to Thy faithful, who trust in Thee, Thy sacred sevenfold gift.

Grant the reward of virtue ; grant at the end salvation ; grant everlasting joy. Amen. Alleluia.

Power and tranquillity, majesty and gentleness, rapture and calm, joy and consolation are the breath of the Holy Spirit. The noble and classic glory of the plain-song in this hymn to the Spirit—what a melting note it takes on, trembling away into the ineffable ! It can be likened only to the fine-traced rays of a Gothic rose-window.

Through the Spirit of God, who has been " poured out on the children of adoption," " the whole orb of the world exults in profusion of joy " (Whitsuntide Preface). The Church's liturgy is a service of joy. The Greek liturgies lay special stress on the joy that the Holy Sacrifice awakes in us. Before the last blessing in the Liturgy of St. John Chrysostom the priest recites a final prayer :

" O Christ our God, who Thyself art the fulfilment of the Law and the Prophets, and who hast fulfilled the whole dispensation of Thy Father, fill our hearts ever with joy and gladness, now and always and to all eternity. Amen."

Repeatedly the liturgies of East and West pray for peace. The *pax Christi* is the glorified, heavenly life of our Lord, which rejoices us. Peace is our life in the Spirit. The peace of God blossoms out of the Holy Sacrifice. The Eastern Mass-ritual calls the Eucharistic service the " oil of peace." As an introduction to the solemn prayer the deacon calls : " Let us stand orderly, let us stand reverently, let us see that we offer the holy oblation in peace." And the choir answers : " Oil of peace, a sacrifice of praise." Then the priest blesses the " holy people " with the words : " The grace of our Lord Jesus Christ, and the charity of God the Father, and the fellowship of the Holy Ghost be with you all."

And does not the Latin liturgy know how to beg for peace ! *Pax Christi* shines over all its prayers and actions. " The peace of the Lord be always with you," the Church calls to us at one of the sublimest moments of the Mass. Earnestly the Church prays for the precious possession of holy peace : " Grant, O Lord, peace in our days, for it is no other that defends us but Thou, our Lord and God." *Dona nobis pacem* is our prayer as pilgrims. When the Church implores peace so perseveringly, when she stretches out her hands so longingly to the " King of Peace," then in the peace of Christ there shines on her the great, deep, spiritual miracle of the new life. The " Kingdom of Peace " is the new, glorified state of the world ; yes, in the peace of Christ the world sees the great harmony of all the voices of heaven and

earth in the one endless love-song of the Holy
Ghost. Leo the Great in a Christmas sermon
calls peace " the repose of the blessed in the
abode of eternity." In peace we are already in
contact with the heavenly glory of the next
world. Before the priest and his ministers
exchange the kiss of peace at a solemn High
Mass, the priest and deacon kiss the altar
together. That is a symbol of the spiritual
Christ and His saints, the heavenly Church.
One with Christ, one with the Church in
heaven—we too all wish to be one in a sacred
peace. The peace of Christ is a transfigured
communion : but communion is possible only
in the Holy Ghost. Peace is the " fulness of the
Holy Ghost." Many of the Eastern liturgies
pray after the consecration for the *pleroma*, the
fulness of the Holy Ghost ; and the significance
of this prayer seems to be the same as that of
the prayer for the peace of Christ, " which
surpasseth all understanding " (Phil. 4 : 7).
Peace is the new message of a new world. *Pax
Christi*—these words are written on the walls of
the catacombs, over the graves of the martyrs,
over the early Christian basilicas and the
monasteries of the West. The peace of Christ is
our life, and in the peace of Christ we die. The
peace of Christ exults in the children of peace.

It gives us the "wings of a dove," that we may seek and find the day without evening, the peace of the everlasting sabbath. " O Lord God, give us peace (for Thou hast given us all things)—the peace of rest, the peace of the sabbath, which has no evening. . . . For then Thou wilt so rest in us, as Thou now workest in us. . . ."—" My life shall wholly live, being wholly full of Thee."—" O Lord, our God, Thou hast called us ! We call unto Thee ! We hear Thy call—hear Thou our invocation ! Complete, O God, what Thou hast begun. Forsake not Thine own ! Amen " (St. Augustine, Conf. xiii, 35, 37 ; x, 28 ; &c.).

VI

CONSUMMATION IN GOD

The German mystics speak of the consummation
of the grace-endowed soul in the depths of God's
unity. This view is the application to the grace-life
of the doctrine of the cyclic movement and reciprocal
indwelling of the divine Persons. Conformed to the
unity of the divine nature, the soul comes into a
proprietary relationship with God, so that God and
the soul belong to one another, God pervading the
soul through and through and perfecting it. The
liturgy speaks of a holy exchange between the divine
and human natures, which attains its ultimate
reality in the Holy Eucharist. Mystical theology too
is familiar with the soul's consummation in the
" transforming union " with God.

VI

" A NOBLE-HEARTED man, who with simple composure attends to the meaningful word that the eternal Son spoke in the gospel : ' Where I am, there shall My servant be also '— one who has not shrunk from that ' where ' which the Son in His humanity assumed when dying on the Cross, but who has shared that holy ' where ' in the fellowship of the Cross— such an one may quite well and rightly enjoy, after a ghostly manner and with much gladness, in time and eternity, so far as that is possible, the happy abode of the pure sonship of God in His bare divinity. And where is this abode of the sheer godhead ? It is in the figured light of the divine unity . . . where in dim indeterminateness all multiplicity ceases, where the mind lays aside its self hood and all conscious activity of the self. Thither the spirit climbs spiritually, to the suprarational place of the secret bosom of God. . . . What greater wonder can there be than the bare divine unity, wherein the trinity of the Persons merges by reason of simplicity, and where all multiplicity of selfhood is annulled ? This is to be understood in the sense that the emanation of the Persons who are

93

poured forth returns ever into the unity of the selfsame being. . . . That bare divine unity is a dark stillness and a silent rest, which no man can understand unless the Unity Itself enlighten him. . . . The distinction of the Persons severally is not perceived in that simple modeless mode. For neither the Person of the Father, taken by Himself, gives beatitude, nor that of the Holy Ghost : but the three Persons, cohering in unity of essence—that is blissful consummation."

These Words of Blessed Henry Suso produce the same quiet effect that surrounds one in a lofty Gothic cathedral — an inward emotion soaring up in stone. The noise of the world's business sounds endlessly far away. Every sound that is caught in the vast precincts undergoes a peculiar rhythmical transformation. Here is the place of sheer stillness. Every word, every sound is so to speak disembodied, etherealized, spiritualized. But the very stillness and silence here is a hymn ; a tide of melody rises that speaks to us of deep and wonderful things —most of all when the light plays about the pillars ! The great sheaves of stone flame as with unearthly gold, throw off all their inertia, and rush heavenwards, to the shoreless sea of the godhead.

German mysticism has been likened to the Gothic cathedrals and its period has been called the Gothic period. Certainly much of the lofty spirit of Gothic art is found in the great spiritual movement of the Middle Ages, which produced its finest flowers especially in the Rhineland. These holy flights, this impetuosity of the spirit outbidding itself, this love for the transcendent, this noble passion for the supreme and ultimate that we find in German mysticism—all this reverberates in the Gothic harmonies in stone. But most of all this losing of oneself in the infinite, in the ethereal spaces of God. The masters speak bold words about it. All of them—Eckhardt, Tauler, Ruysbroek, Suso—tell of the " supreme passage " of our created, grace-endowed mind into the wondrous depths and secrecy of the godhead ; they speak of our entering into the " inward silence " of the divine unity, where " the distinction of Persons is no longer perceived," where God " dwells in uncreated light." Here in the secret unity of the divine nature, where all is repose and perfection, the soul too is mysteriously perfected. It plunges into the interior, unfathomed depths, into the ocean where all streams find their resting-place. " They who live in God are sunk in God, in the divine essence, where the Persons inhere in the substance where pure Being is " (Eckhardt).

According to the German mystical teachers our spiritual life consists not only in our being mysteriously taken up into the vital processions of the Trinity, not only in our having life from the Father through the Son in the Holy Ghost ; rather the soul that is united with God is introduced by God Himself into the inner recesses of His divine unity, where Father, Son and Holy Ghost are one God in the ever-blessed one and holy Essence. There the soul lives in the perfect, wondrously deep repose of God ; there it becomes itself " simple and modeless " and evanesces in the glad tremors of a holy possession of God. Is this doctrine but a play of mystic fancy, an idle exaltation of mystic thought, or have we here one of the profoundest truths of our grace-life ?

If we put this question to the mystics themselves, they refer us to the " holy doctors." They refuse to state for us any doctrine of their own. St. Thomas, the Victorines, Peter Lombard, then St. Augustine, but above all Dionysius the Areopagite, are their masters. The last-named has spoken perhaps most profoundly of all of the soul's entrance into God and its assumption to uniformity in the obscurity

of the godhead. Indeed, his whole thought,
as that of the German mystics too, rests on the
idea of the mystic cycle : God, the One, brings
all things back to unity. This idea is no " neo-
Platonic invention " ; it is even biblical. For
have we not the words of our Lord in St. John's
Gospel : " I came forth from the Father and
came into the world : again I leave the world
and I go to the Father " (John 16 : 28)?

The image of the circulation of divine life
dominates the whole Middle Ages. Peter Lombard, whose theological commentary on the
" Sentences " became *the* dogmatic manual of
the Middle Ages, built up his entire system on
the conception of the cycle. Theology in
general is familiar with a cyclic movement in
God. The eternal processions in God, which
determine the differences of Person, flow back
to their origin. The relations in God are relations of communion. It is precisely that by
which the divine Persons are distinguished,
wherein they are at the same time mutually
related. We worship in the Unity of Trinity and
in the Trinity of Unity.

God the One is the Triune. The infinite
wealth of the one God unfolds itself in a three-
personal possession, without losing itself : for
the three divine Persons, who possess the one

nature identically, with a difference of relation only, are by this very difference so linked to one another that the Trinity implies the Unity and the Unity the Trinity. The supreme property of the Father is to be the origin of the Son and the Holy Ghost. He is so orientated towards the two divine Persons who proceed from Him, that He simply cannot be conceived without Them. The property of the Son is to have life from the Father and in common with the Father to breathe forth the Holy Ghost. And the Holy Ghost's special property is to receive the one, identical divine life from Father and Son together. But the divine relations are also one and the same thing with the eternal processions in God. Here we stand in awe before the wonderful intimacy of the divine life. Our understanding cannot penetrate this mysterious obscurity ; we can only confess in astonishment that the Unity in God unfolds the Trinity and yet again that the Trinity points to the inner abode of the divine Unity.

As we have already seen, the eternal processions flow back (according to the view of theologians) in the cycle of the divine life into the abyss of God's unity. This one nature is the deepest and inmost principle of the mutual compenetration of the divine Persons. The

Latin Fathers understand this reciprocity, this absolute inwardness of the divine outgoings, as an exuberance of God's unity and call it " circuminsession " (reciprocal indwelling). God the Father, Son and Holy Ghost permeate one another mutually. While the Son proceeds from the Father, they nevertheless remain in each other. The eternal processions are wholly inward, an immanence of the Persons by reason of the one divine nature. And our life, too, is to be included in this reciprocal indwelling, this joyful, mutual possession. The Greek Fathers regard this holy compenetration of Persons further as a mysterious cyclic movement (perichoresis), which originates from the Father, flows through the Son to the Holy Ghost, and returns into the bosom of the divine unity. They regard the divine unity as the supreme goal of the vital movement in God, just as it is their origin. Indeed, they see in this compenetration of Persons an eternal, blissful finding of Themselves in the unity of the divine nature, a mysterious establishment of divine communion. This one divine essence, in which all movement comes to rest, is the holy place where all yearning and desire are stilled.

The soul which under the inspiration of the Holy Ghost lifts eyes of faith to the summits of

99

this one, thrice-holy essence of God, is illumined by the snowy radiance of the divinity. A new world is disclosed to that soul—a land of wonders opens its gates. We believe that the great masters of German mysticism have opened those gates for us. Their sublime doctrine of our mystic intercourse with the divine nature is nothing but the teaching of the Greek Fathers on the cyclic movement in God logically applied to the life of grace. Does not St. Peter's phrase take on a new light for us here— that we are made partakers of the divine nature ? (2 Pet. 1 : 4.)

It is not merely that the traits of the divine nature are in some way impressed on the soul supernaturally : rather the grace-adorned soul is here so caught up into the secret unity of God's essence by the cycle of divine life, that it shares *after its own fashion* in the wonderful perfection of God's life, and—as far as is possible for a creature—enters through the Trinity into the Unity and through the Unity into the Trinity. " Grace is a spiritual heaven, in whose calm and wondrous depths God secretly consummates His perfect works " (Eckhardt). Yes, our being too is comprehended in this interpenetration of the divine Persons : " As reciprocal indwelling is predicated in Holy Scripture not only of the divine Persons among Themselves, but also of God and Christ in His humanity, and even of God and creatures in the state of grace, one can speak of a perichoresis even in the two latter cases " (Scheeben).

We may surely think here of the wonderful prayer at the mixing of the wine and water at Mass, which expresses this species of perichoresis by grace : " O God, who didst wonderfully form the dignity of human nature, and still more wonderfully didst re-form it, grant us by the mystery of this water and wine *to become partakers of His Divinity* who deigned to partake of our humanity, Jesus Christ Thy Son, our Lord, who with Thee liveth and reigneth in the unity of the Holy Spirit, God for ever and ever." Or the Mass-prayer on Christmas night : " May the offering of to-day's Feast be acceptable to Thee, we pray, O Lord : that by Thy bounteous grace we may through this most holy intercourse be found in the likeness of Him in whom with Thee is our substance " (Secret Prayer for the First Mass on Christmas Day).

The Holy Eucharist is surely the last and deepest expression of this life in one another of Creator and creature. It is no mere presence of the Lord, no mere entrance of the God-Man into us ; it is also an assumption of our whole being into Christ, an insertion of our mortal life into the glory of immortal life, a marvellously intimate continuity of life with Christ. That is why eucharistic communion produces that invisible state of a lasting communion with God, the knowledge of which is the delight and happiness of the blest, and the reality of which is announced to us in Jesus's own words : " He that eateth My flesh and drinketh My blood, abideth in Me, and I in Him " (John 6 : 57).

This " perichoresis," however, is of course only a reflection of God's wonderful intercommunion ; it is a " belonging to one another mutually of God and the creature " (Scheeben), a penetration of man by God. *We cannot penetrate God, but God wants to penetrate us through and through.* We are in God. " God is the location of the world," says a religious thinker. But our being in God is, by reason of this gratuitous collocation in the divine orbit, as we saw, a living and moving in the hidden depths of the divine unity.

The words of St. Paul, " in Him we live and move and are " (Acts 17 : 28), although they refer primarily to the omnipresence of God, receive their final fulfilment here. The dwelling-place of the Christian is God Himself. " The angels are they who stand before God, but men are they who rest in God." These words of a mediæval ascetic express doubtless our consummation in the inner splendour of the one divine essence, radiant with triune light. We seem, however, from this point of view to understand better not only German mysticism but also an obscure and mysterious doctrine of mystical theology, which—particularly since St. John of the Cross—speaks of the inward consummation of the soul " in transforming union," a union which elicits " a humble peace " in the perfected soul. This highest degree of union with God is founded on the grace-life of the soul. It is the full development of the life of grace, and not a grace reserved to a few chosen souls only. All the children of God are called to immerse themselves in this tranquil sea. The grace of transforming union is, according to the avowals of the mystics and the teaching of spiritual authors, so perfect a repose in God that the soul rejoices in a constant upward look towards God and is pervaded in all its activity by the continually transforming presence of God. A " slumber beside springs of water " is what St. Augustine calls this mystic state of lasting possession of God. We understand that what is here described is the final consciousness with which the sanctified soul becomes aware of its mysterious absorption in God. It is then filled to overflowing with the joy of God's nearness, and haunted by the sweetness of the divine music within itself. God Himself has brought the soul home, and nothing more can trouble its peace, for like Mary it remains at the Lord's feet.

So the mystics look on our life as a holy pilgrimage, a journey whose end is the inner unity of God. The more a soul keeps itself open to God, abandons itself to the mysterious action of God and lets itself be caught in His current, the deeper God draws it into the secret abyss where all springs rise. In grace, therefore, which contains every glory in germ, lie possibilities yet untold. God perfects the soul of him who gives himself up to God. The meaning of Christian perfection therefore lies not in mere development of personality, nor merely in the cultivation of all one's spiritual and moral faculties, nor even in the religious direction of our life alone—our aim, the end and summit of our evolution lies in the interior of God, among the incomprehensible mysteries of the divine nature, which even now holds our being in its embrace. Our way is a transformation—a transformation into the Light ! Of that which takes place in the quiet and secret recesses of union with God, no human tongue can speak worthily. The ways of the saints might tell us something of it : that curious strangeness of religious people in this world, the wonderful repose, the calm, divine peace which beams from them, gives us some slight notion of the rare marvels that God would fain work in us. The Christian approaches ever nearer to that perfection which is already established in him essentially, " for this is the will of God, your sanctification " (1 Thess. 4 : 3).

VII

LIFE IN THE RICHES OF GOD

Our life in the interior of God gives us a share in
His riches, which are unfolded in the multiplicity of
His perfections. The cardinal perfections, which
contain in their abundance the various attributes,
are Unity, Truth and Goodness, and these are
ordered according to the Trinity.—God's royal
Unity is seen operative in His supreme simplicity,
which is purest spirituality and freedom. This unity
of God, which is all-encompassing and lifted above
space and time, is eternity.—God's Truth is brightest
clarity, and lives in the eternal Wisdom which unites
knowledge and life.—Wisdom is the supreme value
and the supreme good, its essence is goodness. The
Goodness of God, which lavishes itself in love,
breathes the wonderful Beauty of God ; while the
fragrance and the whole glory of God's goodness
resides in His absolute Holiness.—As far as is possible,
the soul, elevated by grace, partakes in its own
fashion in the attributes of God. In particular the
Eucharist, once again, is the source of this divine
life in us, and the Church's liturgy is an expression
of this glorious reality.

VII

GOD'S love draws us into God's interior. God is our goal. In Him is the deepest fulfilment of our being. God is, therefore, the riches of our soul. God's riches are an infinity of glory. Timidly, and only in the consciousness of our creaturely poverty, do we venture to look up to the heights of God, to the holy mountains which burn in the triune light.

God's wealth is His one, absolute, indivisible reality. And yet we cannot draw out for ourselves the fulness of God's being otherwise than by decomposing it successively into the rays of its several perfections or attributes. That is a bold venture indeed for the believing mind! But God Himself of His unfathomable goodness has in His divine revelation resolved, so to speak, the uniform, white, burning light of His divinity into the multiple colour-harmony of the divine attributes. The clearer God's attributes appear to the enlightened eye, the more the veils are lifted which conceal the invisible essence of God. For God's essence and His attributes are one and the same thing! Although, therefore, " the distinction of Persons is not perceived here " (Suso), yet the splendour of the Trinity is reflected like a very subtle radiance in the order of the divine attributes. For since the divine Persons compenetrate one another in the unity of Their nature, They convey the august characteristics of the Trinity into the motionless divinity of Their sheer being. Only from the height of the trinitarian viewpoint can we gain some faint understanding of the glory of the one divine Substance. We, therefore, follow the " Seraphic Doctor," St. Bonaventure, whose divinely enlightened perception detected the triune note in the order of the first great attributes of God. Although Unity, Truth and Goodness, which theology calls the transcendental attributes of God, pertain to each of the three Persons equally, yet unity is ascribed specially to the Father, truth to the Son, and goodness to the Holy Ghost. We attempt in what follows to attach the various attributes to these fundamental perfections, which are ordered according to the Trinity, by showing how in the symphony of God's attributes the grand motif of Unity, Truth, Goodness dominates.

Our way into the interior of God is, as we have learnt, an ever more deeply realized participation in the divine nature (2 Pet. 1 : 4). The

divine nature, however, is the vehicle of the
divine attributes. When our soul enters into
the sublime bright-darkness of the one divine
substance, there takes places its gratuitous
" assimilation " to God. This assimilation by
grace unfolds the riches of God in the soul.
Man so elevated is not merely to receive in
general a supernatural being and life : rather
he is to become himself, as far as that is possible,
a mirror and reflection of the several divine
attributes. The perfections of the divine
essence tend to pour themselves out, as it were,
over souls and to imprint on them the features
of God's countenance.

First of all our spirit is immersed in that
august *unity*[1] which theology names as the first
of the transcendental attributes of the divine
nature. God is " the primal One." He is
absolute unity, the fixed point, the inmost
centre of being, in which all its radii are a profoundly mysterious, superessential unity. This
unity of God is unique and unapproachable.
The circle is but a feeble symbol of God's unity.
Resting in itself, perpetually beginning and end
—or better, knowing neither beginning nor
end—always alike, always self-supporting—it

[1] Transcendental Unity is here (as already indicated) considered
as an attribute of the divine nature, whereas in the preceding chapter
the divine nature itself was so designated.

is an image of the infinite changelessness of
God's eternal cyclic movement. God is indeed
the Alpha and Omega, the " royal unity," in
everlasting self-possession ; the totality of
beginning, totality of maturity, totality of consummation, subsisting in Himself, the eternal
centre of His own orbit. A superarithmetical
unity, beyond enumeration, this unity is the
inner principle of all numerical evolution : it
is All-unity. God's unity is infinite perfection of
being. " Unity of totality," He is called—
simultaneously one and all. The One and the
All, the secret aspiration of Platonically minded
religious thinkers of the pagan world, is
realized in the Christian idea of God. God is
" the sole One," and thereby also the eternal
and original measure of all becoming. " This
simple and sheer Being is the first and supreme
cause of all causal being. By the simultaneity
of His presence He encompasses all temporal
becoming as beginning and end of all things.
He is at once in all things and outside all things.
Therefore a wise doctor says : ' God is as a
circle whose centre is everywhere and whose
circumference is nowhere ' " (Suso).

The absolute unity of God is no cold exclu-
siveness ; though proper to all three divine
Persons in like manner, it is the original

principle of all life, a principle which we worship especially in the Father. Nicholas of Cusa, whose universal genius loves ever to immerse itself in the all-fulness of the divine unity, and who sees here the last and deepest idea, the structural model of all Catholic thought, calls God the " composition " (*complexio*), and also the " coincidence of opposites " (*coincidentia oppositorum*). As the point of intersection bears within itself figuratively all lines, so God's unity bears within itself, while essentially ordering, the rich variety and contrariety of all movement.

God is the harmony (*concordantia*) of the universe, the simple and actual " involution of all that is evolved." Therefore God is the " greatest " and at the same time the " least." Because God is the greatest He must also be the least ; even the smallest thing is therefore great in God ! For with God all measure fails ; in Him is the original measure of all measures.

Nicholas of Cusa develops the thought in this way : the greatest must also be the least ; for if the greatest were not also the least, it would not be something which it could be, and therefore it would no longer be the greatest. Anyone who takes this reasoning as if it were strict logic, and is not acquainted with mediæval dialectics, may perhaps see nothing here but a playing with empty concepts. But if we listen for the distinctive note of this particular world of thought, we shall be astonished to discover the profound reverence of this religious mind in face of the Ineffable and Eternal. What is vital here is the ultimate insight of the typical religious man that God is beyond all our logical processes; that we can indeed speak of Him and that our words correspond to something true, but that they are only an indication, a signpost. God is the " greatest " and the " least " : this antinomy means that God is neither " great " nor " small." He is above the whole sphere of concepts, and yet the meaning of all concepts is true only in God. But that can only be grasped from God outwards— that is, supernaturally. "God is the greatest" then means : God is " everything," " the fulness of things." And " God is the least " means : God is absolute oneness, the most inward and real centre of being. One and all, least and greatest now postulate each other mutually.

The ideas of Nicholas of Cusa were understood thoroughly and carried further by the talented thinker Görres. He refers to the numerical unit, which comprehends all numbers. The unit is the root of all numbers ; it is posited in them and comprises them all in itself. Similarly God is the first and original Reality, which in its creative unity contains the archetype of all orders and substances in itself. God is the primal Unity, which cannot be deduced from anything else, and towards which all things point. Indeed, we must call God the Super-unity : He is beyond all classification, and He is deeper than the deepest roots of thought. Because He is raised above all categories of measure and value, He includes everything in Himself. The greatest and the least are equivalent for Him. He is greater than the greatest ; and since the least is the root, model and measure of the whole, God is also less than the least that can be imagined. In His wonderful oneness God is " the supreme centre," which bases all things in itself.

Görres expresses these thoughts in the preface to a book on the life of Jesus. Christ, the God-Man, is for him, as for Nicholas of Cusa, a manifestation of the *complexio oppositorum* : God and man, the greatest and the least at once, glory in the garment of poverty, the King of life dying on the Cross. Christ is the divine manifestation of the " One, who is All," the Word made flesh, who contains everything by which the created worlds are constituted.

Holy Scripture again and again uses similar
antitheses in speaking of the incarnation and
life of Jesus. St. John particularly has a flair for
them. From this point of view the Cross is the
deepest revelation of this mysterious contrast.
We see in the Crucified the King of Glory, and
in Him who is crowned with thorns the Lord
of the World. The Greatest becomes the "least."
" I am a worm and no man "—the psalmist
makes the Lord pray on the Cross (Ps. 21 : 7).
But this descent into the deepest abjection is
made only that all things may be fulfilled.
The Cross is the " yoking together of height and
depth," of God and the world ; it is the plan of
all Christian existence. In Christ is revealed to
us the whole mighty span of the divine unity,
which—while subsisting wholly in itself—yet
embraces all things in love and contemplation.
Here, indeed, we touch on an essential con-
struction of Catholic thought, a fundamental
law of our holy faith : precisely because God
is highest, absolute transcendence — precisely
because He dwells in inaccessible light—for that
very reason He can become " all things " ;
because He subsists immutable in Himself,
without shadow of change, He bears the arche-

type of created forms eternally and substantially in Himself.

In God the soul rests in the fulness of life. If the soul in its bare nature is, according to the mediæval doctors, "somehow all things," how much more is the child of God " all things " in Him whom it addresses as " my God and my All ! " In God the soul acquires uniformity. All contingency finds for the religious man its deepest and ultimate idea in God. From God outwards he judges the multiplicity of created being. All acting, willing, thinking of the redeemed man unfolds itself from an inward principle, as an emanation from a being united with and transfigured in God. A supernatural, serene repose shines over everything. The holy mystical doctors speak here of the " repose of the soul's powers " in God. The nearer we approach to God, the more our soul is filled, heaped up with the riches that flow from His unity. He who possesses God, say the Fathers, has everything at once in the One. All gifts come to him with God. How infinitely the soul is then enlarged in God ![1] True piety broadens. It gives to the soul that fineness of feeling for

[1] It seems to us necessary here to return once more to the immensity of God and our entrance into His immense life, because we are here regarding immensity as founded in God's essence, whereas in the fifth chapter (" Life in the Spirit ") we treated only of the force of love enlarging us in God.

all that is good and noble, that awed receptivity for every genuine value. It endows a man
with a sensitive and kindly habit of understanding and forgiving, which we admire so
often in the saints. What happens is that God's
being, which is Immensity, bursts the narrow
bounds of our heart, and immensity, this
infinite majesty, becomes our portion. And in
the noble breadth of God, in the oneness which
is all things, in this innermost interior of God,
all things meet in hallowed proximity and there
takes place that secret exchange of life and
cognition which far surpasses all concepts and
even all consciousness.

We have seen already how this wealth of God,
this " one and all," has come nigh to us in
Christ—how it has become *ours*. St. Paul has
expressed this in the Epistle to the Ephesians,
which is literally saturated with the idea of the
fulness of God in Christ. He sees love as the
force which brings us to God, which pours out
God's riches in us : " I bow my knees to the
Father of our Lord Jesus Christ, of whom all
paternity in heaven and earth is named : that
He would grant you, according to the riches of
His glory, to be strengthened by His Spirit with
might unto the inward man : that Christ may
dwell by faith in your hearts : that, being

rooted and founded in charity, you may be able to comprehend, with all the saints, what is the breadth and length and height and depth, to know also the charity of Christ, which surpasseth all knowledge : that you may be filled unto all the fulness of God " (Eph. 3 : 14–19). It is this love of Christ that we grasp in the Sacrament of the Holy Eucharist.

This mystery of the " One " that is " All "—how it shines out from our Lord's eucharistic presence itself ! According to Dionysius the liturgy, the Church's holy service of love to the Eternal, with all its forms, sounds and melodies, and more particularly in its sacramental dignity, is a coming forth of the One—who nevertheless remains ever in His majestic oneness—in order to bring home the many into the bosom of primal Unity. The eucharistic presence of the Lord is a glorious reflex of the divine unity which irradiates His transfigured Body. But the reason of this dispersion of unity in multiplicity of forms is to bring the " all," the scattered ones, home into the abyss of calm light where God is " all in all."

The Church, as the One Lord in the many members of His sanctified Body, is a mystery of the " one and all." The ancient liturgies speak time and again of this all-oneness of the

Church, which grows up out of the eucharistic food. From this point of view we gain a deeper understanding perhaps of the Church's liturgical chant, plain-song. Oneness of spirit, transfigured rest in God rings through its restrained richness. But the oneness, which is shown outwardly in the very unison of voices, is not rigidity, but abundance—amplest and loftiest abundance. For it is just one of the grand features of plain-song that with few and simple musical resources it gives expression to many things, the very fulness of things. But we have not really to do here with a psychological mode of expression. Plain-song is a vibration of divine and spiritual forces, which rise from the depths of redeemed man's God-enlightened consciousness of union. Plain-song is the hymn of the entirety, the community and its great, moving mystery-realities ; and yet again it is truly the hymn of the individual, but of the individual who in the Church becomes " all things " ; that, indeed, as we saw, is the joyous consciousness of the Christian—to have become at once " all things " in God.

The oneness of God as deepest source of the community of Christ's Body the Church, which overflows melodiously in plain-song, is also the prime model of all Christian art—as

Desiderius Lenz and the Beuron school have clearly seen. The simplest form, the prime model contains all perfection and fulness. This idea of lofty restraint, composure of line, makes itself strongly felt in the aristocratic form of the Roman liturgy. We think that the Roman Church as an expression of the " community of love " is quite specially a representation of the divine unity.

The unity of God, source of all evolved riches, is, as inmost point of concentration, absolute *simplicity*. The Fathers call God " the bright darkness." For He is above all conception and understanding. He who soars to God must leave all things behind. All thinking and willing, all seeking and yearning is powerless to reach God in His infinite simplicity. Our reason can indeed know with certainty God's existence and attributes, but this knowledge is rather a knowledge of what God is not than of what He is. Our deepest knowledge of God is that we cannot comprehend him—it is our patient, worshipping silence.

For God is incomprehensible! That is why there is no " concept of God." God cannot be confined in a concept. There are only thoughts of God, which approach the divine essence reverently from afar. He who would know God must enter with Moses into the cloud ; there it may be that the face of the Incomprehensible will turn to him and the rays of His glory play about Him as he worships. He who is in grace is himself a thought of God, which bears upon it the brightness of God's countenance, and whose life, too, is incomprehensible in the Incomprehensible. God's incomprehensibility is the reflection of His absolute, most luminous simplicity. God is the purest nobility, spiritual " selfhood," as the mediæval thinkers put it. God is unthinkably beyond all composition. The simpler, more uncompounded and uncomplicated a spiritual being is, the nobler and more excellent it is. Our words are too heavy to express the nobility of the divine essence. God is nobility itself. He is metaphysical simplicity. In Him is purest rank. But—and here the mysterious dialectic of the divine being is again revealed—just because God is unapproachable simplicity, because He dwells in most inward selfhood, because He is the Impenetrable itself, for that very reason He can penetrate all things and be the innermost core of every being. Of divine Wisdom it is written : " She reacheth everywhere by reason of her purity " (Wisd. 7 : 24).

Now the nearer a soul comes to the pure

being of God and the more it is lit through with the rays of divine purity, the more God's nobility envelops it. God is the nobility, the rank and title of a soul that is visited by grace. The redeemed man lives in the noble purity of God. The mediæval mystics love to speak of the noble breeding of the Christian soul. In their eyes the graced soul is sprung from the royal light and wears a diadem more splendid and costly than all the kings of the earth. In God its being has become finer, clearer and brighter than the sunbeam. The soul is so to speak simplified in God. Its powers are more clearly and radically co-ordinated. It views all things as it were with God's eyes. The more spiritual a man becomes, the simpler he becomes and the more clearly stand out for him the great fundamental lines of being. He sees how all orders and values are grounded in God and how the universe rests in Him. To be simple means to see all in one and to operate accordingly. The whole nobility of the soul lies in its simplicity.

If God is the highest, noblest simplicity, then He is absolute, purest *spirituality* : for God is the Super-spirit. All our human words are much too encumbered to be applicable to God ; and yet the pure sense of all words is found only in the " Word " which is God Himself. We must be ever transcending our conceptual images in order to adapt them even remotely to God. God is known only in God. Faith knows Him. When, therefore, theology speaks of God, it is really not the intrinsic value of the words that brings us nearer to God, but the ring of faith in them, their eternal sense. Only the believer who loves feels the inward secret, the free, dematerialized reality of all the words of God. Only he who is of God hears the words of God (1 John 4 : 6).

Because we are of God, we can speak of God —for we know that God's language is understood by the " enlightened," the " initiate." For that reason we also dare to predicate of God the word " spirit," that " word of man's longing " (Lippert). Only we know that God is the Original Spirit, far beyond all created spirituality—and yet also the eternal ideal, the source of all spiritual culture. This transcendent spirituality is reproduced in the soul by similitude in the supernatural life. Only now does the soul become truly spiritual. To lead a spiritual life means to live in the super-reality of God, to breathe the eminently spiritual, pure life of God. " Where the Spirit of the Lord is, there is liberty " (2 Cor. 3 : 17) ;

the Spirit is free, unhindered mobility. God is spirit, He is that wonderful agility itself. Wisdom, we are told, is " a versatile spirit." He who is in God is in freedom. The glorious liberty of the children of God is the flowering of divine freedom in the soul. How the Fathers have sung again and again the praises of this freedom ! Only when we are " taken captive in the Lord " are we freemen of God. Being bound to God is therefore being born into freedom.

The Church's mysteries are the doors which lead us into the wonderland of the spirit and freedom. The Christian, nothing less than he, is the free man, and the Church the " free-born " that springs from the majesty of God. The Eucharist is the food of spiritual freedom. It is the Bread of Angels, of the children ; it nourishes us with heavenly freedom. The Holy Eucharist, which makes the Body of the Lord and the great Deed of the Lord sacramentally present in the " mode of existence of a spirit " (Scheeben), lifts us clean above the bonds of time, up into community with the free spirits who sing the " Thrice Holy " before the throne of the Almighty.

The Greek Liturgy expresses this sublime idea of our union with the free, heavenly world in the Mass-procession, the Great Entrance as it is called. While the Offerings are carried solemnly to the altar, the choir sings : " We who mystically represent the Cherubim and sing the Thrice-holy hymn to the life-giving Trinity, let us put off all earthly cares, for we are about to meet the King of all, invisibly escorted by angelic hosts." We are, as the Armenian Liturgy says, " fellow-servants with the angels and saints." The holy service of the Spirit allows us to stand in the angelic choir, raised high above the erring ways of this earth. The Eucharist is indeed the victory, the divine triumph of the spirit and of freedom. In the Eucharist mere earthly categories are superseded. Christ is truly and really present under the species, though not in the manner in which extended bodies are present, but in the intensive mode of pure spirits.

This divinely spiritual presence of the eucharistic Christ (according to Scheeben a kind of participation in God's omnipresence) is the source of our immortality. The Eucharist is immortality itself. The Missal prayers speak often of the Eucharist as immortality or the food of eternal life. For the Fathers, therefore, a man is not " immortal " until he has become a eucharistic man, that is, one who has been deified by grace through the Mysteries. " Immortal " is not understood here in the philosophical sense : philosophical or natural immortality is an endowment of every soul once it is created. But our true immortality is a mysterious birth into the abyss of God's immortality.

The more spiritual a being is, the more free it is from the bonds of time and space. God as the most spiritual reality is essential transcendence of all temporal order. Source of the spiritually immortal life of the creature, God is in fact super-immortal—that is to say, God is *Eternity*. Eternity is not merely the negation of time, it is rather the immutable, independent possession of spiritual life. In God there is no change, no passing away. Subsisting in indivisible, spiritual, pure unity, He does not realize His existence by stages, like the creature ; for indeed He is the absolute presence of all reality. He possesses Himself eternally in full perfection. In possessing Himself He bears within Himself the spiritual archetype of all becoming. For God there is no succession ; He is everlastingly present in identical fashion to the remotest past and to the future. He is the fixed centre of being, and all becoming in the time-series is as the circulation of the waves that go out from Him. So God's eternity is at once the origin and term of all time. Eternity is present in its full, God-like perfection to each and every section of the temporal process. All succession of time is but as a remote image of that triumphant reality which pulses through God's ever-young eternity. And God's eternity is our inheritance.

We would fain adore and be silent ! The God whom our forefathers for thousands of years have called the Eternal, who is Eternity itself, who measures the span of the ages, to whom the furthest past and the future is completely present, whose footsteps echo equally through all ages, who is God "from eternity to eternity," whose one, infinite gaze embraces whatever is bound to the wheel of change. the Lord of all ages and eternities—He Himself is to be our " life " ! He Himself is our exceeding great reward. He speaks to us thus : " Yea, I have loved thee with an everlasting love : therefore have I drawn thee, taking pity on thee " (Jer. 31 : 3).

If the thought of eternity weighs on the natural man with a religious terror, to the Christian it should be sheer joy. The Church in her liturgy is ever hymning the " eternal God." Eternity makes harmonies of joy and peace in the Church's prayer. God's eternity is our pride. For God's eternity is love. Only love is eternal. To love alone it is granted never to fall away.

In grace men touch the threshold of eternity. Grace is the seed of eternal life, say the theologians. The New Testament overflows with it. We have only to open the Epistles of St. Paul or of the Beloved Disciple : the words scintillate eternal life, the melody of the *vita æterna* touches our hearts.

Wherever there is a religious man, there eternity begins. Born of eternal love, known to God's eternal gaze before all time, we carry eternity in us—a precious treasure in a fragile vessel. The eternal life, however, whose germ is planted in us by grace, is not merely perpetual life, but a mysterious immersion in God's own personal eternal life which is above time.

As we are included in the eternal life of God, as we are bearers of eternity, so too eternal life should flow from us : " He that believeth in Me, as the scripture saith : Out of his belly shall flow rivers of living water " (John 7 : 38)—" springing up into life everlasting " (John 4 : 14)—says our Lord. " In me is no love of perishable things, but pure water that calls home to the Father "—is the cry of St.

Ignatius, the " God-bearer," exulting in the immortality of the Spirit of God. Our whole life, then, is a translation into time of the divine, radiant vision of eternity which surrounds it.

Since then the gates of eternity are now thrown open to grace-uplifted man—the Epistle to the Hebrews speaks of the access of Christians to the inviolable mountain of Sion—therefore we are joined in hallowed communion with those who have " gone before " us, who have " through the changes of times past pleased God " (Oriental liturgies). We are united with the patriarchs, prophets and martyrs, with the apostles and saints and the just of all ages. Eternity, indeed, is in us. It is like a great, undivided, self-consistent stream, which evolves from itself the events of all time and leads back again to the first principle of all occurrence, into the immovable rest of the eternal God. This divine rest is our portion. Time and again the Fathers speak of it, of the wondrous immutability of God, which inwardly perfects the Christian soul. The meaning of our life is to rest ultimately in God, who is rest motionless and undisturbed—rest that transcends all activity and passivity alike. It is at once complete and absolute life and absolute stillness,

unmoved action and active immobility. And
this is our salvation—to find rest in the rest
of the Unchangeable. St. Augustine has col-
lected these thoughts in a profound prayer :
" Highest, best, mightiest, most merciful and
most just, most hidden and most present, most
beautiful and strong, steadfast and yet not to be
grasped, immutable and changing all things . . .
ever active, ever at rest, gathering and yet
needing nothing, supporting and fulfilling and
protecting, creating and nourishing, perfecting,
seeking though nothing escapes Thee ! Thou
lovest, but without passion ; Thou art jealous,
but without sadness ; Thou repentest, but
without pain ; Thou art angry and remainest
calm ; Thou variest Thy actions but never Thy
decree. . . . ' Say to my soul : I am thy salvation ! ' Speak clear ! Behold, O Lord, the ears
of my heart ; open them and say to my soul :
' I am thy salvation ! ' I will hasten after that
voice and will take hold of Thee. Hide not Thy
face from me ; I will faint away and die, that
I may not die, but may see Thy face."

* * *

We seek the face of our God. It is the voca-
tion of men to be on the way, to be pilgrims
towards the inaccessible light of the eternal sun.
But who can gaze on the sun, on its scorching

brightness ? The sun is an image of God and of
His bright, burning truth. All the truth that
the eyes of the soul, thirsting for light, drink in,
is only a sunbeam, not the sun itself. And yet,
too, truth does meet us in every true word. All
that is true speaks of Him, signifies Him, the
eternally true, without being able to reach Him
and express Him. God is *Truth*. But truth is
ineffable. Though all tongues tell of her, none
can confess her. Only God Himself can speak
of Himself. Only the Ineffable can give testimony of Himself. This self-expression of the
Inexpressible is that eternal " interior Word "
(Logos) which before the beginning of time
rises in the bosom of the Eternal Himself as the
Word of His truth, and is the hidden Face of
God. And therefore we too are to live by truth.

Immersed in Him who says of Himself : " I
am the Way, the Truth and the Life " (John
14 : 6), we are sanctified in the truth, consecrated for the truth. " Sanctify them in truth ;
Thy word is truth " (John 17 : 17)—was our
Lord's petition in His high-priestly prayer.
Therefore we too dare " with open face " (2 Cor.
3 : 18) to look on the splendour of eternal truth.
Yet how can this be possible ? How can mortal
man make bold to endure the burning brightness of the sun, and not die ? " I will die, that I

may not die " (St. Augustine). He who would enter the light of truth must know how to die— how to die to self and get away from all images and modalities that hide God's image. " The smallest image of the creature is as big as God " —says a master of interior contemplation— "for it takes from thee a whole God." God would possess the soul entirely ; so the soul must become quite empty, quite free for God. Every created image, even the smallest, can hide God's presence from the soul. He who would grow rich in God must become poor, he must get away from his own idiosyncrasies and all created images. The seers of the spiritual life, therefore, speak over and over again of going out from all creatures and entering into God. When God seeks entrance, the soul must place itself in the sheer immobility of God. It must retire into itself ; for there in its own inner depths it finds the happy realization of eternal Truth itself.

St. Augustine has given expression to this mystic experience of the soul : " Late have I loved Thee, Beauty so ancient and so new, late have I loved Thee ! And behold, Thou wast with me ; but I was without and sought Thee there . . . Thou wast with me, but I was not with Thee . . . Thou didst call and cry out to me and didst break through my deafness ; Thou didst flash and lighten and didst drive away my blindness ; Thou didst send forth a sweet odour and I breathed it and do pant after Thee; I tasted, and do hunger and thirst ; Thou didst touch me, and I was inflamed with desire for Thy peace " (Conf. x, 27).

God Himself must speak. He alone can break through the deafness of our heart. All contemplation of truth, therefore, rests on the " interior voice of God." God expresses Himself in the soul, and the soul is then inflamed with longing for God's holy peace. All contemplation grows up from attention to God's mysterious voice. " I will hasten after this voice and will take hold of it ! " (St. Augustine). But wherever a man seizes the truth, he is first seized by it. God's truth contemplates itself in us. And as we stand in its view, the majesty and splendour of Truth ever young and ever new is formed afresh in the inward man.

Philosophers call truth a correspondence between thinking and being. God is the absolute unity, the sheer identity of thinking and being. He is at once being and thought. The truth of God is the being of God inasmuch as in thinking it comprehends itself. Therefore God's truth, as we saw, is the expression of the Inexpressible. And so also the grace-illumined man can catch God's self-expression within him and bear God's Word within himself. Christ is the Expression of God, the manifestation of that which is hidden from eternity. Here again our concepts are too dull and inert to give complete expression to this. Because God subsists wholly in Himself, just because He is beyond all access, He can without losing Himself make the Word of His truth to be heard.

Here again may we not see the mystery of God's transcendence of being? Supreme remoteness of being is the cause of the deepest affinity of being, for God alone can reveal Himself in loving condescension without renouncing His absolute supremacy. When God expresses Himself, He raises the creature to Himself. It is just here that we find ourselves in an entirely divine, supernatural sphere, in which only divine laws hold good. While God, the True One, expresses Himself in Christ, so that we in prayerful reverence know Truth itself in the Lord, He wishes to express Himself also in the many, the redeemed who are mysteriously incorporated with Christ. To know God's truth is therefore to have the witness of God in oneself. " He that believeth in the Son of God hath the testimony of God in himself. . . . And this is the testimony, that God hath given to us eternal life ; and this life is in His Son. He that hath the Son hath life. He that hath not the Son hath not life " (1 John 5 : 10–12).

Since we rest with the Son in the bosom of the Ineffable, since we have God's witness in us, we are to be also God's witnesses. This puts in a new light the words of our risen Lord : " You shall be witnesses unto Me " (Acts 1 : 8). A prophetic splendour shines round every Christian life. We understand in this sense the words of St. Peter on Pentecost Day : " This is that which was spoken of by the prophet Joel : ' And it shall come to pass in the last days (saith the Lord), I will pour out of My Spirit upon all flesh : and your sons and your daughters shall prophesy : and your young men shall see visions : and your old men shall dream dreams. And upon My servants, indeed, and upon My handmaids will I pour out in those days of My Spirit : and they shall prophesy. And I will shew wonders in the heaven above and signs on the earth beneath . . .'" (Acts 2 : 16–19). The days of the great prophecy are come. Every Christian who has life lives by the Truth. He is a word of God.

He is essentially a prophet. And we—what else can we do but, with the Queen of Prophets, keep the words of God in our hearts (Luke 2 : 51) ?

When we give testimony of the Ineffable, we ring in harmony with the self-utterance of God ; knowing the Invisible, we partake in His eternal self-contemplation. God can only be known in God. God is the Invisible, whom no creature can behold with the eye of nature in the sublimity of His being. All images—even the subtlest mental images—fall short of God. He who would see God must be rooted in the truth. God Himself must be the mental image by which He is perceived. In the heavenly vision the blessed are so immersed in the light, the substantial truth, that they see God with God's eyes, face to face. All fluctuating, earthly knowledge is but a road to that. But yet our supernatural knowledge in faith, and in the mystical contemplation that is founded on the divine virtue of faith, is a life sustained by God's truth. We are already in the lap of truth ; but our contemplation of truth is still wrapped in the venerable obscurity of the god-head. It is not yet knowledge face to face. But the enlightened soul comes ever nearer to this wonderful immersion in the luminous taber-

k   137

nacle of God. Theologians describe supernatural knowledge as an assimilation to divine truth ; truth itself is the motive of the grace-knowledge of God. If the blessed contemplate the deity within the deity, if their vision has become in some way uniform with the one divine self-vision, the contemplation towards which every Christian soul strives—although it is a true and real vision in God—is still more truly a fragmentary knowledge, a shining forth of the divine sun in the diverse rays of its truth. *As long as we are here on earth, we do not see the divine essence immediately in itself.* But as the rose unfolds itself in its petals, so the mystic rose of God's being shines out for us in the blossoming splendour of the several truths of faith. These divine truths are known immediately by the grace-enlightened soul, and wherever the soul's admiring gaze rests on the mountain-chain of these spiritual realities in revelation and dogma, wherever it recognizes them in the " symbolic light " of created things or traces their outlines in the universe, there it is in silent, thrilled contact with the " imageless godhead " itself.

Because our Lord is Truth itself, He is also the " true God." What is the meaning of this invocation *Deus verus*, " true God," on the lips of the praying Church ? We are filled as with a victorious, mighty force, as with a triumphal hymn of strong joy, whenever we call God the " True One." That God is the True means : God is the one substantial, super-substantial God, as the Fathers describe Him. In God alone does our life become a true, substantial life, a real life. The aged martyr bishop St. Ignatius yearns for the " setting of this world and the rising in God " : for then only, when he is wholly with God, will he be " a true disciple."

That God is the True means also : God is the absolutely Faithful one, whose gifts of grace are given without recall. We know ourselves to be in the shelter of His incomprehensibly true reality. His truth shields us. He who rests in God rests on the bed-rock of everlasting faithfulness. God is the immovable foundation of the being of the faithful. He says of us : "Touch ye not My anointed !" (Ps. 104: 15). To touch the children of God, one must first touch God. The Psalms are a hymn to this strong reality and fidelity. *Veritas* in the psalmists' speech means faithfulness, truth and reality. The old Roman Church knows much of this. The *Ecclesia* is the " Elect," she who is confirmed in the truth of God. The oldest collects in particular reflect this deep sense of strong and joyful security which springs from the truth of God. *Deus verus* is our perfect confidence. We can say with Holy Scripture : " The joy of the Lord is our strength " (2 Esdras 8 : 10).

God's truth is as a calm and unfathomable lake. Most clear and bright and diaphanous, God is *clarity* itself and at the same time the depth of all mysteries. Truth and clarity live only in God. All earthly things are too gross, all created things—even the spiritual creation —too complex. Clarity is the light-giving power of eternal truth. Clarity lives in the wondrous arrangement of God's truths, in the coexistence of the several truths in the luminous circle of God's absolute truth.

Therefore God's clarity shines forth in His sole and eternal Son, the image of His most pure and radiant being. The Logos is the clarity of God. He is the fulness of God's ideas. In wonderful order He gathers the entire riches of those ideas in Himself. He is the *Ordo Trinitatis* —the ordering principle, instinct with clarity, of the Most Holy Trinity.

Since God is the sole Transparent one, no created eye can see through Him. Such an organ, as we have already learnt, is too dull to comprehend that most pure and subtle clarity of light. Only God's clarity itself can see through all. The maximum of transparence and clarity is the same as the maximum of light. God's clarity is the burning, flaming, and yet so fine and placid light-centre of being.

To be near to God is to live in the light. We are the children of the light, who should show forth the wonderful clarity of God's glory. Our works should give testimony to the light, to the Father of light : " You are the light of the world. A city seated on a mountain cannot be hid. Neither do men light a candle and put it under a bushel, but upon a candlestick, that it may shine to all that are in the house. So let your light shine before men that they may see your good works and glorify your Father who is in heaven " (Matt. 5 : 14–16). When our Lord speaks of the " clean of heart " He surely includes those who bear within them the clarity of God, the " illuminated," who are wholly transparent to God, whose hearts are lit up with the rays of God's majesty. As the pure clarity of God is impenetrable to the world because of its inner delicacy, so the children of light are to the world an abstruse mystery. The world comprehends not what is of the Spirit—they are removed from the world's

eyes, their life seems often mere foolishness—
and yet they bear the traces of God's clarity
within them.

Clarity is allied to the classic. The classic is
that which is objectively great, ontologically
ordered. All order that springs from within,
that is rooted in being, is clear and lucid. The
prayer of the liturgy is thus clear and lucid,
orderly and unconstrained. How wonderfully
transparent are the collects of the Roman
Missal ! Here clarity and depth are at one.
" Classic restraint " is not mere strict objec-
tivity, it is not frigidity nor mere hierarchical
form. Here, joined to clarity of thought and
form, is dogmatic profundity, and yet also a
certain free and blithe ease of address that is
quite peculiar to the " play of the liturgy."[1]

Again we would point to plain-song. Clarity
sings in it. Its pellucid rhythms plunge us into a
depth and richness inexhaustible. The " classicism " of plain-song is not to be explained simply
from antique elements of style ; in the " divine
classicism " of eternal clarity we find the
original type of church music.

Divine truth, the " ideal or archetype of all
things, the measure and foundation of all ideas,
rules and laws " (Scheeben), appears in Holy

[1] *Cf.* Guardini : *In Spiegel und Gleichnis*, Mainz, 1932.

Scripture as the life-giving Wisdom of God. God's truth is *Wisdom*. The God of Truth is not merely the essentially clear Intellect, raised high above all the hierarchy of creation, the pure and self-contained Thought, the primal Thought that is completely real, the one sheer identity of thought and being : the God of Truth is also the Wise God.

Wisdom is creative truth, truth whose thoughts are things. In wisdom are rooted the divine ideas which are the eternal types of all being and becoming. While God contemplates Himself, His divine and eternally clear glance comprehends simultaneously in Himself the deepest source and origin of created things, the prototypes of all those derived realities which are unfolded in space and time. The foundations of created form rest in God. All things have in God an eternal aspect. They are only thoughts of God which have become cosmic, have been realized in time. The wisdom of God is the mysterious unity of all the ideas of God, the coexistence of all those eternal patterns of things created. The thoughts of God, which comprise all that is in any way possible and all that is realized in being and becoming— an infinite gradation of hallowed lights—are eternally existent in God's wisdom and therefore

are not independent entities but identical with
His essence.

Again we find ourselves in wondering adoration of the riches of God's thought. An immense world, spiritual and pure and completely real in God, opens before us. Every
created thing, projected into the fluctuating
region of the perishable, bears within itself an
eternal mystery, grows as it were beyond itself,
finds its ultimate explanation in the eternal
ideas which God's love has conceived.

God's thought bursts the bounds of pure
intellect : it is creative and vital. The true God
is also the living God. Wisdom is the queen and
mother of all life, wisdom is life : " He that
shall find me shall find life, and shall have
salvation from the Lord " (Prov. 8 : 35)—so
speaks Wisdom in the old dispensation. She is
love. Every thought of God is love. So, too,
it is Wisdom's whole delight " to be with the
children of men " (Prov. 8 : 31). Only in love,
then, is wisdom apprehended. The sapiential
books of Holy Scripture always emphasize the
unity of truth-perception, love and life.

He who receives wisdom in love, knows God.
Wisdom brings about that enlightened, rapturous experience of God and divine things of
which the mystics speak. One who is a child of

God has Wisdom for a holy friend. Because she
is the mother of creation and because the germs
of being and life spring from her, he who loves
Wisdom views through her the mysterious
feature of God in the mirror of created values
and orders. Wisdom can only be obtained by
prayer. She is the sacred gift that is bestowed
on us as the most precious of all goods. The
Church, therefore, makes us beg for wisdom in
the Breviary prayer : " Give me, O Lord,
Wisdom that sits by Thy throne. . . . Send her
forth from the seat of Thy majesty, that she may
abide with me and work with me " (Respon-
sory at Matins in August).

*   *   *

Wisdom is the divine power which fixes
values, which unites being and value in the
highest degree. As highest value she is the
highest good, whose essence is to impart itself
ad infinitum. " All good things came to me
together with her "—according to the poet of
the Book of Wisdom (7 : 11).

God is the highest good, and therefore also
the height of *goodness*.[1] The higher and more
perfect a spirit is—say the theologians—the

[1] On the goodness of God compare also what is said of love in the
preceding chapters.

more absolutely and perfectly he desires to communicate himself. God, the highest of all goods, the Original Good, desires to impart Himself in loving abundance. Therefore the holy Apostle says : " God is charity " (1 John 4 : 16), and God's charity consists in this, that He " hath first loved us and sent His Son to be a propitiation for our sins " (1 John 4 : 10).

The inner principal of all communicability lies in the cyclic relation of the three divine Persons. Unceasingly flows the stream of loving largesse from the Father to the Son and from Father and Son to the Holy Ghost. But the tide of this love desires as it were to overflow beyond itself. The whole supernatural order is but a development, a continuation of this self-imparting goodness of God.

As highest good and purest goodness God is the most lovable good. The sapiential books lay stress on this union of God's supreme perfection, absolute truth and all-compelling, self-effusive love. Under the symbol of Wisdom the divine essence is sung in the fondest and sweetest strains. As " mother of fair love " (Ecclus. 24 : 24) Wisdom pours forth the rivers of life (Ecclus. 24 : 40). Yes, God's essence—that almighty, creative force—is according to Holy Scripture a sweet, beneficent, gentle, kindly,

pure and subtle Spirit (Wisd. 7 : 22–23), which
" conveyeth herself into holy souls and maketh
them friends of God and prophets " (Wisd. 7 :
27).

The goodness of God in its gentle fervour of
generosity rests in the Holy Ghost. Although
goodness is essentially proper to the divine
nature, the Holy Ghost, as the Outpouring of
divine love, is more especially the personal
vehicle of God's goodness.

They who live in God live by goodness. God
alone is " the Good One." " One is good,
God " (Matt. 19 : 17). If God is in us, then
`` substantial goodness " itself is in us. In grace
we attain to a truly unutterable dignity and
elevation. But if Goodness itself is in us and we
are united to the highest goodness, then our life
too must be one stream of holy oblation. The
saints are life entirely self-dedicatory. The
nearer we are to the centre of the divine sun,
the brighter and purer must that sun of Goodness itself radiate from us. The redeemed are
light-fountains of goodness. He who would be
good must place himself in the divine, solar
light of eternal goodness ; he must let the
current that flows from God and leads back to
God flow through himself.

God wishes to impart Himself through us.

147

We are called to be a reflection of His goodness. We are to diffuse God's love over souls. That is why according to the saints perfect happiness consists in the giving of oneself. One who loves in God, one whose being has become lavish goodness, loses nothing, but gains all things. Here our Lord's words are verified : " He that shall lose his life for Me shall find it " (Matt. 10 : 39). God's goodness is the supreme good which, though given up, surrendered, is never diminished. Prodigality is the law by which goodness grows. One who is captivated by the goodness of God must himself become a spring of goodness whose waters can never fail.

If God, as Scripture says, is love, then all His attributes too are radiations of love ; they are the wonderful refraction, so to speak, of His communicative, open-handed goodness. The goodness and love of God, in which and with which all His sacred attributes are one, celebrates in its adorable harmonies and symphonies the praises of divine *beauty*. When Holy Scripture speaks of God's beauty, it is like a song of triumph, a canticle : " The Lord hath reigned, He is clothed with beauty " (Ps. 92 : 1). " Strength and beauty " are His raiment. Surrounded with light He walks " in the beauties of holiness " (Ps. 109 : 3). " The sun and the moon . . . shall go in the brightness of Thy glittering spear " (Hab. 3 : 11).

Beauty is unity in multiplicity, it is " the unfolding of the power and riches of inward perfection and life " (Scheeben). The beauty of God is the eternal new song that sounds in the bosom of the Trinity. Here in the interior life of the Trinity is perfect unity and multiplicity, here is the eternal signification of all hidden beauty : the absolute simplicity of the divine essence, the one nature that subsists in three holy, coequal Persons—unity and totality at once, unison in concord, riches developed in absolute order and inward consistency.

How God's beauty shines forth in Christ, whom we call " beautiful above the sons of men " (Ps. 44 : 3). His life on earth shows us the winning beauty of God. Even His Passion is clothed with the purple of love, the purple of His most precious Blood. It is thus that the Church has seen Him in the great ages of Christianity. She sees even the suffering Saviour in the radiance of spiritual beauty : the Man of Sorrows shows forth the sublime beauty of God's suffering.

And this royal beauty of God invests the sanctified soul. Bathed in God's purple splendour we are a marvellous spectacle to the

angels and saints. The soul is invited to take
its fill of the beauty of God. " I shall be satisfied when Thy glory shall appear" (Ps. 16 : 15),
says the psalmist. Glad indeed are we made
by the knowledge of God's pure and shining
beauty, the ultimate ideal of all beauty in the
creature. The very existence of this beauty
fills the religious man with an exalted joy.
But in divine love the soul may have inward
experience of God's beauty. Of this beauty of
God, which we enjoy in His love, St. Augustine
writes : " But what do I love, when I love
Thee ? Not corporal beauty nor temporal
charms, not the brightness of this daylight so
pleasing to the eye, not the sweet melodies of
divers songs, not the perfume of flowers and
unguents and spices, not manna and honey,
not limbs acceptable to carnal embraces. Not
these do I love, when I love my God. And yet
I love a kind of light and a kind of voice and
scent and food and embrace of my inner man :
where there shines unto my soul what space
contains not, and where that sounds which time
bears not away, and that smells which no
breath scatters, and that tastes which appetite
does not diminish, and that clings which reple-
tion puts not away. This it is that I love, when
I love my God " (Confessions x, 6).

From sunrise to sunset the Church sings the hymn to God's lovely beauty. The eucharistic mystery itself, indeed, is the great song of the most beautiful of the sons of men. Here lives the all-harmony of love, which unites all the voices of heaven and earth. "Heaven and earth are full of Thy glory." And the *gloria Dei*, the hidden splendour and beauty of God, is unfolded in the sacred rite. In the eucharistic meal the " hungry " are filled with that bread which contains in itself all sweetness of God. The words of Scripture are fulfilled : " They shall be inebriated with the plenty of Thy house : and Thou shalt make them drink of the torrent of Thy pleasure " (Ps. 35 : 9). But the hymn to God's beauty is the hymn to God's holiness.

. The *holiness* of God is the radiance, the fragrance, the glory of His goodness and beauty. Theologians say that God is substantial Holiness. He is holy because He is absolute goodness and beauty. Who can comprehend the infinite preciousness, the ineffable dignity of the divine essence ? God's holiness is incomprehensible. No human tongue can express it. All that the divinity contains of sublimity and splendour—and we confess in amazement that it is endless Infinity itself—all that forces us to our knees in adoration at the awe-inspiring wonder and the purity and perfection of divine goodness and majesty, all this plenitude of the *mysterium tremendum*, is God's holiness. And all that is most divinely subtle and delicate and imponderable, all that sends thrills of joyous fervour through us whenever we so much as pronounce God's holy name—that inexpressible, tremulous vibration, the enkindling and effervescence of the heart which God visits— all this is a breath of His loving holiness and holy love. The angels, those mighty and glorious spirits who are smitten through with the flashing fire of God's purity, who stand as the great lights before the throne of the All-holy, who are the " flowing light of the god-head," whose spiritual eyes plunge exultant into the primal flood of all mysteries—even they cannot but veil their faces again and again before Him to whom they cry without ceasing : " Holy, holy, holy is the Lord God of hosts."

In this ecstatic praise from the hosts which marshal their choirs above all the heavens to the glory of God the Holy One, the Church joins when she performs the sacred service before the Lord. Holiness enwraps us at that moment.

This sanctity of God is felt in a specially pronounced manner by the religious world of the

East. It seems to be God's will that East and West should complete one another in their religious characteristics. While the West with its classic Latin liturgy—as we have already noticed—represents particularly the unity and truth of God and shows us the shining face of the Word, over all the prayers and ceremonies of the Eastern Church lies the spirit of divine holiness. In shuddering awe, and yet too in joyful, serene consciousness of our participation in God the Holy, she sings her songs of thanksgiving to the " holy, strong, immortal God " :

" Let us send up a hymn, ye nations,
    To our God who worketh wonders,
    Who delivered Israel from bondage ;
    Let us sing the song of victory and rejoice :
    We will sing to Thee, the Master, the only
        Lord.
    Ye faithful, let us all in hymns
    Magnify the uncreated Trinity,
    Which ordereth all the immaterial hosts of
        the heavenly choirs,
    And let us cry : Holy, holy, holy art Thou,
    O God the Ruler of all !
    In the beginning of Thy works Thou didst
        make, O Creator of the angels,
    The incorporeal substances which surround
        Thy stainless throne,

153

To exult before Thee : Holy, holy, holy
    art Thou,
O God the Ruler of all ! "
And this All-holy One, who ever seeks and
possesses Himself, clothes us with the purple
robe of His divine glory. The Fathers call grace
also " holiness." If He is holy by virtue of His
essence, we are so by grace. But grace is a
participation in the All-holy. Therefore, grace
is a life in the abyss of God's dignity, majesty,
radiant perfection and plenitude. The " redeemed " is a " holy one." Every child of God
is an awe-inspiring mystery, because the
majesty of God shines out from him. " If thou
dost not call thyself holy, thou art ungrateful to
the Lord " (St. Augustine). The New Testament, too, refers constantly to the faithful as
the " saints " : " But you are a chosen generation, a kingly priesthood, a holy nation "
(1 Pet. 2 : 9).

Holiness is here understood not as ethical
perfection, but as a mystical, super-real assimilation and community with the All-holy. There
is a substantial holiness, of which the foundation
is laid in baptism. This substantial holiness is
also the form, the inner effulgence of all the
perfection of a child of God, all growth in
perfection.

Whoever would become perfect—and all Christians ought to wish it—must know first of all that " holiness " is our very substance. This is what St. Paul was ever fain to say to his believers : " But you are washed : but you are sanctified : but you are justified, in the name of our Lord Jesus Christ " (1 Cor. 6 : 11). " There is now, therefore, no condemnation to them that are in Christ Jesus " (Rom. 8 : 1). But all holiness is grace upon grace. Christ is to us holiness, Christ is to us justification.

To become holy means to let " the Holy " grow within one, to ripen to the full age of Christ. We are called to holiness ; and we must listen to the call of God. God has called us "unto sanctification" in Christ Jesus. How serene must we then become, how inwardly glad and free ! It is the will of the great, almighty God that sanctifies us. We can do nothing except let His holy, summoning, forming, electing, divine will be done in us. God has prepared, foreseen, and predestined our life from eternity. We dare not therefore seek ways of our own to holiness. All lies secure in the solicitous love of God, which has seen and ordained every day of our life and growth and all the laws of our development, until we have become conformed to the Son of God. " . . . As

He chose us in Him (Christ) before the foundation of the world, that we should be holy and unspotted in His sight in charity : who hath predestinated us unto the adoption of children through Jesus Christ unto Himself, according to the purpose of His will : unto the praise of the glory of His grace . . . " (Eph. 1 : 4-6).

When we appear every morning before the face of the Holy One, we stand on a " holy mountain," as a " holy people." On the face of the Church at prayer and on the face of each of the redeemed beams the noble brightness of the holy God. When Moses came down from Mount Sinai he bore on his face the reflection of God's light, and the people could not endure its brilliance. And yet this brilliance was but a shadow of that light which so gloriously transforms our being. " Now if the ministration of death . . . was glorious, so that the children of Israel could not steadfastly behold the face of Moses, for the glory of his countenance, which is made void : how shall not the ministration of the spirit be rather in glory ? For if the ministration of condemnation be glory, much more the ministration of justice aboundeth in glory " (2 Cor. 3 : 7-9).

And when we receive the Bread of Angels, on which rests the brightness of God's counten-

ance who comes to us, to whom we sing with
the angels in the *Gloria* : " Thou alone art the
Holy One, Thou alone the Lord, Thou alone
the Highest, Jesus Christ, with the Holy Ghost
in the glory of God the Father ! "—then,
indeed, we have the source of holiness itself
within us.

In the Oriental Mass-ritual, when the priest
calls the faithful to Holy Communion, he says
in a loud voice :

" The Holy to the holy ! "

And the people fall on their knees and
respond :

" One is holy ! One is the Lord ! "

Yes—One is holy ! One, who sanctifies us
also in a holy repast which is the pledge of
eternal glory.

This divine food is our strength on the way to
the heavenly Sion ; it brings us ever nearer to
the light of that day when we shall not only
sing the *Sanctus* in company with the hosts of
heaven, but when, ourselves consummated in
the bosom of God, we shall share one life with
the hallowed *Sanctus, Sanctus, Sanctus.*

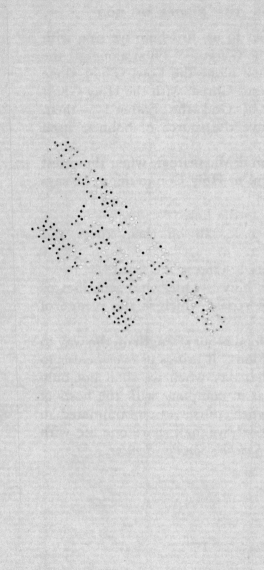

PRINTED IN GREAT BRITAIN BY
THE ALCUIN PRESS LTD.
WELWYN : HERTS.